The Fragile Blossom

By the same author

The Fragile Blossom:
Crisis and Change in Japan

Between Two Ages:
America's Role in the Technetronic Era

Dilemmas of Change in Soviet Politics
(*editor and contributor*)

Alternative to Partition:
For a Broader Conception of America's Role in Europe

Political Power:
USA/USSR (*with Samuel P. Huntington*)

Africa and the Communist World (*editor and contributor*)

Ideology and Power in Soviet Politics

The Soviet Bloc—Unity and Conflict

Totalitarian Dictatorship and Autocracy
(*with Carl J. Friedrich*)

The Permanent Purge—Politics in Soviet Totalitarianism

Political Controls in the Soviet Army
(*editor and contributor*)

THE FRAGILE BLOSSOM

Crisis and Change in Japan

by Zbigniew Brzezinski

HARPER TORCHBOOKS
Harper & Row, Publishers
New York, Evanston, San Francisco, London

 For information address Harper & Row, Publishers, Inc., 49 East 33rd Street, New York, N.Y. 10016. Published simultaneously in Canada by Fitzhenry & Whiteside Limited, Toronto.

A hardcover edition of this book is available from Harper & Row, Publishers.

First HARPER TORCHBOOK edition published 1972

STANDARD BOOK NUMBER: 06-131698-9

Contents

Introduction

THIS BOOK is a personal report on Japan. Derived in part from impressions acquired in the course of a six-months' stay in Japan during the first half of 1971, it is an attempt to sum up my conclusions about that country's prospects, domestic and international.

I went to Japan on a Ford Foundation grant (which I gratefully acknowledge) to explore the likely role that country may play in international affairs in the coming years. I did so, not seeking to become an "instant expert," but because I felt that it might be useful for a nonexpert, interested broadly in foreign affairs, to become better acquainted with this important Asian nation. Since Japan's role in world affairs cannot be separated from Japan's domestic scene, I first had to reach some judgments concerning the likely changes in Japan's domestic, social, political, and economic conditions. As a result, this report addresses itself to one broad question: How is Japan changing, and what are the implications of that change domestically and internationally?

The answer, I must reiterate, is both speculative and analytic, offered by a political observer with limited prior familiarity with Japan (confined largely to frequent but very brief visits), certainly not even remotely an expert on Japan. My report, therefore, is not an attempt at a study in depth; it would be pointless for me to try to match the excellent works available by a number of American experts on Japan.[1]* My hope, however, is that my other work may have given me some additional perspectives and experience relevant to this task.

It might be useful, by way of background, to indicate briefly how I approached the subject and what I was trying to find. In preparation for my stay in Japan, I devoted the fall of 1970 to background reading and to extensive travel to South Korea, Australia, and Indonesia. In all three places I met and talked with cabinet members, various officials, economic planners, the military (especially, of course, in Indonesia), and intellectuals. I also gave some public lectures and interviews and conducted a number of seminars with high-level officials of the respective governments.

Early in 1971 I settled in Tokyo, where I had a similarly active program. In addition, I traveled to South Korea, Taiwan, and Singapore, where I discussed Asian affairs in general and Japan in particular with various high officials and intellectuals.

In my conversations I tried to explore the following questions with regard to domestic issues: Is the pattern of Japanese politics changing? If it is, what are the likely implications of that change for political stability? For Japanese democracy? How deeply rooted is the Japanese democratic system? Is there an ideological shift underway in Japanese politics and in the Japanese value system? Is a new nationalism emerging in Japan, and, if so, what is "new" about it? How is it likely to express itself domestically and externally? What are the key groups upon which Japanese

* Numbers refer to a section of Source Notes beginning on page 143.

democracy is dependent, and what factors in general point for the continuation of Japanese democracy? What are the principal threats to it? What have been the key factors prompting Japanese economic recovery and rapid growth? What are the key problems likely to confront Japan's economy in the next five years? Over which of these problems does Japan have autonomous control? How far is liberalization likely to go? How can Japan protect itself against international instability affecting Japanese markets and sources of raw material? Is a changing value system likely to affect Japan's economic allocations and, in turn, Japan's economic growth?

With regard to external issues, I tried to establish what it means to speak of a new balance of power in Asia and how such a balance will affect the American role. What do the Japanese mean when they speak about Japan's new global role? What sacrifices is Japan likely to make in pursuit of such a role? What are the Japanese goals in promoting development assistance to the less developed nations? What role do the Japanese see for themselves in Asia, and should Japan have a special role in Asia? What is the likely pattern of Japanese-Chinese and Japanese-Soviet relations in the course of this decade? What do the Japanese think about the implications for Japan of a possible United States withdrawal of forces from Japan by 1975? Is such a withdrawal desirable from the Japanese point of view? How would it affect, from the Japanese standpoint, the reliability of American nuclear protection? What would such a withdrawal mean for Japanese rearmament? Considering likely economic problems (domestic reallocation, labor shortage, political opposition), what form might Japanese rearmament take? How will Japanese rearmament affect relations with China, the Soviet Union? Will Japan go nuclear?

I do not pretend to have found the answers to these and many of the other questions that arose in my discussions with the Japanese, but the above indicate some of the general lines I pursued, naturally in varying emphases, in the course of my different discussions. Many of these questions perplex the Japanese themselves, and they raised them as often as I did.

During my stay in Japan I became increasingly skeptical of straight-line economic projections as the basis for forecasting Japan's likely future and increasingly impressed, not only by the obvious interdependence of the different aspects of Japanese reality, but also by the high degree of Japanese dependence for their success on circumstantial factors essentially not of their own making and often beyond their direct control. As the general title of my report suggests, I found the sudden blossoming of Japan to be something very fragile—a matter worthy of very careful cultivation by the Japanese and of very sensitive attention by Japan's friends abroad.

Let me conclude this introduction by noting that whatever I may have learned about Japan was facilitated by the unfailing courtesy and kindness of my several Japanese friends and hosts. I went away profoundly attracted by many aspects of Japanese life and with a sense of real affection and admiration for the Japanese. As all people do, they have their faults and shortcomings, but they do have—it seems to me—a unique capacity for blending reflection and action, for promoting even in the context of a highly dynamic society "a universe of the spirit, in which everything communicates freely with everything, transcending bounds, limitless."[2] This quality became more apparent as I got to know individual Japanese better, and I do feel that it gives Japanese society those special qualities of endurance and transcendence without which its recovery might not have been as impressive. I also feel that this vital social cement will be more severely tested in the years ahead, as Japanese society enters a phase of greater complexity—both in the definition of its goals and in the handling of its resources.

ZBIGNIEW BRZEZINSKI

August 1971
Northeast Harbor, Maine

The Fragile Blossom

Part One

Domestic Developments

1

Social Patterns

THE INITIAL IMPRESSION that one obtains from a stay in Japan is that of a highly stable and apparently cohesive society. The social fabric seems to be tightly knit and to fit well both the psychological and more mundane needs of the Japanese. It appears to be responsive to the Japanese desire for a clearly demarcated social hierarchy while providing a ladder for the many who are capable and ambitious enough to climb upward. As a result, most Japanese know their precise place in society—something that enhances their psychic security—and yet also know that they can improve themselves and climb higher.

BEING JAPANESE

In observing the Japanese at work and at play, one is struck by the peculiar combination of an essentially feudal structure with early industrial values. The former is characterized by high deference to established authority, by widespread acceptance of the legitimacy of the very hierarchical order, by an entrenched system of seniority in large corporations (which play a central role in Japanese decision-making), and by an extraordinary cliquishness.* Indeed, the role of cliques in Japanese social, economic, and political affairs strikes a foreigner as a unique feature of Japanese life, making both for effective teamwork when things go well and perhaps for irreconcilable conflicts when they do not (of which more later).

The latter (the early industrial values) involve a strikingly high degree of personal motivation in work habits—something that is visible to the eye when visiting a Japanese office or factory (the employees literally run when performing some tasks requiring moving from one place to another although, characteristically, senior executives walk at an increasingly more stately pace, depending on their position and, given the seniority system, age)—great discipline, extraordinary loyalty to one's firm or business,† and a very high rate of personal savings (which in turn has helped the Japanese banks to assume their central role in Japan's economic life).

This mixture of behavioral characteristics does not make it

* Also by widespread tenacity of old customs. For example, after the fatal airplane crash in the summer of 1971, in which some 160 passengers were killed as a result of a collision between a passenger plane and a Japanese fighter plane, the Japanese public was especially incensed because the surviving fighter pilot—after his arrest—"did not show the attitude of regret or repentance expected of him. Although arrested, he had a good appetite and allegedly asked for comic books. Capping that, the outgoing defense chief, Keikichi Masuhara, was photographed apologizing to relatives of the victims standing upright and wearing shoes when custom decrees that he be barefoot and kneeling" (*New York Times,* August 3, 1971). Mr. Masuhara felt compelled to resign because of the accident—something, unfortunately, that no comparable U.S. official would ever do.

† For a good general discussion of this point, see the perceptive analysis of the Japanese sociologist Chie Nakane, *Japanese Society* (London: Weidenfeld and Nicolson, 1970); Nakane notes that in Japanese the traditional reference to a change of employment "was in terms of 'soiling one's curriculum vitae,' and no doubt this native moral orientation was closely related to the fact that the individual's group identification is formed during the fairly early stages of his career . . ." (pp. 107–108).

easy for the foreign observer to classify Japanese society either as purely traditional or as essentially modern.* Moreover, it gives rise to the perplexing question: Is the fusion of the traditional and modern elements stable, reflecting some unique quality of Japanese society, or is it merely a transitional phase, leading eventually to more open tension between the two?

Before attempting an answer, a few more general observations seem in order. Japanese work habits bring to mind the Protestant ethic, yet it would be a gross error to think of Japan as a transplanted WASPish New England or a Pacific version of Calvin's Geneva. The Protestant ethic applies to work; after work, an altogether different culture takes over, the best Western parallel for which is that of the Mediterranean. It is a culture of play, of drinking and merrymaking for the men. Protestant during the day, Mediterranean during the night, the Japanese seem to com-

* In Herman Kahn, ed., "Comments on Scope, Methodologies, and Format," Basic Public Policy Issues (Hudson Institute, January 1970), p. 8, two useful charts identify the principal characteristics and values of the traditional society and of the North American society:

Traditional Society	*North American Society*
Personal dignity and worth	Worship of success
Family cohesion and loyalty	Cult of the practical and efficient
Social hierarchy and status	Narrow utilitarianism
Spiritual and emotional experiences	Identification of quality with quantity
Emotional and poetic expressiveness	Addiction to sheer action
Propriety and decency	Fascination with the trivial (technical)
Dignified acceptance of fate (or God's will)	Work for work's sake
Tangible and meaningful possessions	Superb dynamism
Scorn for manual labor	Unprecedented diffusion of skills
	Genius for organization and teamwork
	Organizationally flexible and geographically mobile
	Ingenuity, initiative, responsibility and dedication
	Rational utilitarianism

It is really striking the extent to which the Japanese combine both columns.

bine successfully what in the West has involved seemingly incompatible extremes.

Japanese distinctiveness is reinforced by the fact that the Japanese are a strikingly insular people. This is, first of all, a matter of prolonged physical isolation from other peoples, an isolation that—relatively speaking—exists to this day. Surprisingly for such a large nation (over 100 million), very few Japanese citizens are in temporary residence abroad—certainly much less so than is the case with West Europeans or even the Chinese. Also, in spite of the phenomenal explosion in tourism, most Japanese who travel abroad do so to Hong Kong, Korea, or Hawaii, and primarily in somewhat self-contained groups, with relatively little exposure to the "outside" world. According to the most recent estimates, in 1970 approximately 70,000 Japanese were living abroad (almost 40,000 of these businessmen and their families, while Japanese students or scholars studying abroad numbered a little over 13,000 and Japanese foreign service and their families came to approximately 6,500).[1] During the same year, about 936,000 Japanese traveled abroad, with the vast majority visiting the places indicated above.[2]

Closely connected with this insularity and lack of exposure to outsiders is a striking degree of personal insecurity and collective narcissism. When dealing with foreigners, many Japanese give the impression of great uneasiness, which cannot be explained primarily on grounds of linguistic difficulties—after all, the Chinese, who are much more relaxed and self-assured, face the same problem. This sense of uneasiness is accompanied, and perhaps also intensified, by an intense fascination with what the outsider thinks of the Japanese. Such opinions are constantly elicited, and even trivial responses are given wide press coverage and are seriously discussed and evaluated.

All of this seems to reflect a curious ambivalence. While seemingly at ease with themselves and within themselves, the Japanese project an air of insecurity in their relationship to the outside environment and strong inferiority-superiority complexes (the former usually toward the more powerful Western states, the latter toward the less developed Asian countries). These complexes create barriers to close relations with foreigners, but once the barrier is broken the resulting relationship tends to be deeper than is customary among Westerners. A friendship with a Japanese means something.

CHANGING ASPIRATIONS

The element of insecurity in Japanese makeup is intensified by the very pace of change in Japanese society. Insecurity is inevitably generated by the breakdown of established patterns and traditional loyalties, and both are being threatened by the pace of change. Change in Japan involves, above all, very rapid urbanization, prompting increasing physical mobility,* with a corresponding decline in the influence on Japanese life of the much more conservative rural traditions, and the appearance of a somewhat new, uprooted urban working class (prone to extremist appeals); it involves changing life-styles, with a small Western-type apartment, furnished with Western-type furniture, constituting the typical ambition of the young Japanese couple; with increasing prosperity, it involves higher consumption tastes, leading perhaps to lower personal savings; finally, it is beginning to involve growing personal hedonism, a preoccupation with leisure, leading eventually perhaps to lower labor discipline and less motivation.†

* Noriaki Kurokawa, a rising Japanese social planner–architect, estimates in his book *Homo Movens* (Tokyo, 1970) that approximately 8.5 percent, or one out of twelve, of the Japanese move every year—a percentage quite high by Japanese standards, even though still quite lower than the American.

† The five-day week is likely to become a reality in Japan by around the middle of this decade. A survey undertaken by the Japan Productivity Center in June 1970 showed a marked decline among younger workers (from about two-thirds of the workers over thirty-five to about one-third of the workers under twenty-two) in their concern for the prosperity of the companies for which they work.

This change is accelerated and stimulated also by the impact of the mass media, especially television, which reaches almost every Japanese household. With its extensive consumption-oriented advertising and its considerable emphasis on personal leisure, Japanese mass media tend to create new material desires, and also to encourage more widespread imitation of the Western style of life. Slick magazines, sales promotions, massive group tourism campaigns, all contribute initially to a subtle and eventually to a not-so-subtle change in the outlook and way of life of even the average Japanese. Moreover, the young people now entering the labor force already grew up in a consumption-oriented society—the first Japanese generation ever to have done so—and certainly they will be quite different in outlook, discipline, and motivation from their war-ravaged parents or the peasants who moved to the cities but who brought with them their traditional values.

At the same time the intellectual community, even more prone to emulate the West than the masses, is already rather alienated from the Japanese "system," and appears to be suffering from an aimlessness and even intellectual frivolity reminiscent of the "fashionable" left currents in America and western Europe. Intellectually uncreative, its major contribution to Japanese social dialogue is to blend turgid Marxist formulas with the latest American New Left slogans. This renders its real social influence negligible, but it does tend to reinforce the state of unrest among university students. Though the university crisis of the late sixties appears to have subsided—in part out of fatigue and in part out of repression—the university system has been badly hurt and the quality of Japanese higher education leaves much to be desired. Far-reaching reform proposals are to be unveiled in the fall of 1971, with the purpose of streamlining and energizing the university system, and it is likely that in some respects the concept of "elitist" education (abolished after the war during the American occupation) may even be partially restored. If so, it will be a response to the growing need of the Japanese economy for more highly trained personnel, capable of creative scientific innovation.

In any case, the youth represents a factor of great uncertainty insofar as Japan's future orientation is concerned. By 1975 more than 50 percent of the Japanese population will have been born after World War II, and—according to teachers, employers, and social observers—the younger generation appears to be bored, politically indifferent but also potentially malleable, especially if it is swept up by some great emotion.* At the same time, there are indications of a somewhat stronger sense of nationalism among the young, a nationalism not encumbered by memories of defeat and a sense of war guilt, with war films, war stories, and national symbols gaining in popularity.

With respect to social goals, the younger people have already begun to reject the dedication of the older generation to rapid economic growth. The fascination with the GNP, the gross national product—a kind of GNPism as an informal ideology of the older generation—is clearly not as strong among the younger, many of whom take Japan's economic recovery for granted, and some of whom—egged on by the intellectuals and academicians—eagerly adopt the antigrowth doctrines of their counterparts in the Western world.

The postwar outlook of the older people was single-faceted. It concentrated on recovery at all costs, in part because of the dictates of survival, in part because of patriotism, in part doubtless as a way of restoring one's own sense of psychic balance in the wake of shattering defeat. That orientation had many parallels to a phenomenon or mood known among the Japanese as *gashin-shotan*—literally, "to sleep on kindling and lick gall"—a

* Its institutional loyalties are notably weaker than in the case of the older generation. The earlier footnote on company loyalty is paralleled by a similar phenomenon with regard to trade unions.

posture of single-minded determination and forbearance, in a setting of great personal deprivation.*

The younger people, in contrast, have more multifaceted but less clear goals, which include a rather vague concept of the good life, as well as a variety of idealistic social objectives and the already noted greater national sensitivity or even pride. As a result, for many of them—especially for the offspring of the middle class, increasingly flocking into colleges—the growth of the GNP is an insufficient or even unworthy objective. More and more, contrasts are drawn between the GNP and the quality of life, more and more the disparity is highlighted between abstract GNP percentages and concrete manifestations of social inadequacy.

In 1970 the ruling Liberal Democratic party (LDP) suffered major defeats in several key urban political contests (notably in Tokyo and Osaka, Japan's two major cities), and these defeats were clearly prompted by rising dissatisfaction with the social conditions prevailing in the large metropolitan centers.† The

* John Toland, in his *The Rising Sun* (New York: Random House, 1970, p. 109), cites a personal letter from Marquis Kido that explains the meaning of the phrase as follows: "in the dictionary it says: 'to suffer hardships and privations, privations repeatedly in order to take revenge'; however, here it means to ask the people to endure a life of patience and austerity in order to accomplish our purposes. Not too long ago, after the Sino-Japanese war, . . . this phrase was first used in Japan to mean that we were to endure a life of patience and austerity until someday our national strength burgeoned and we would rise again."

† "Only in the provision for mass public transport is the Japanese city ahead of its American counterpart. In every other aspect of social overhead it is well behind, and the asault on the Japanese environment is easily the equivalent of anything Americans know. Moreover, the development of company and government housing is beginning to produce the neighborhoods stratified by income and class long familiar in the United States. School and other differentiations may thus be the next stage" (Marius B. Janson, "The United States and Japan in the 1970s," Gerald Curtis, ed., *Japanese-American Relations in the 1970s* [Washington, D.C.: Columbia Books, Inc., 1970], p. 43). I am not even sure that Japanese public transportation is ahead of the American. Commuter transportation is certainly strikingly overloaded and congested.

terms "pollution" and particularly "public nuisance" (as a synonym for all the various shortcomings in social amenities, ranging from staggeringly poor housing to shockingly lacking sanitation facilities, from polluted air to poisoned water, from inadequate health care to almost nonexistent social old-age care—a problem surfacing rapidly as the extended family declines) are becoming catchall phrases, frequently used in the original English and heard as often in Japanese social-political discussions as earlier one would encounter—also in English—the term "GNP."

It is striking—but not surprising—that some local governments are now beginning to turn against further capital investment, actively opposing the setting up of new plants and increasingly insisting on costly safeguards against environmental pollution. In belated response, central authorities and the top business leadership are beginning to focus on these problems. For example, the Industrial Structure Council, an advisory body to the Ministry of International Trade and Industry (MITI), in a report issued in early 1971, calls for a shift in emphasis from the "singleminded pursuit of growth" to "utilization of the fruits of growth." The report calls for a dialogue with the public in order to reduce and eliminate social frictions and for a considerably expanded investment on social overhead capital, involving almost a fourfold increase in the 1970s, and an additional investment to protect and restore the environment, amounting to about 7 percent of the new industrial investment during this decade.[3]

In the meantime, social problems persist and are in fact getting worse, in part because Japan's growth has been so dynamic that its negative by-products tend to become cumulative and to grow at an exponential rate, while remedies are only now beginning to be undertaken. Moreover, while in general a consensus is emerging that a broadly gauged response is required lest Japan be turned into an industrial wasteland, differences persist as to the extent and character of the needed response.* All of this prompts a condition noted earlier by perceptive students of Japanese life, but somewhat obscured by the international hullabaloo over the spectacular growth rates of the Japanese economy:

> The dislocation and mobility of vast rural populations, the difficult adaptations to urban life, the loss of supporting community and family institutions, the periodic inflation, the unevenness of advance in various sectors, the sharp short-term ups and downs, the inability of housing and amenities to keep up with urban growth, the crowding of schools, transportation and other facilities—all of these will combine to keep aspiration and opportunity continuously out of balance. All of the people will be frustrated some of the time, and some of the people will be frustrated all of the time.[4]

This frustration might express itself in two alternative ways. One would involve a widespread rejection of the existing system, the adoption of the view that the evil by-products of rapid growth are the inevitable consequences of capitalism and of the existing Japanese Establishment, which has a vital interest in perpetuating it, and that the only remedy is a profound renovation of Japanese society. This essentially left ideological position, advocated both by the Japanese Socialist party (JSP) and the Japanese Communist party (JCP)—both of which have lately gained in popular support for reasons indicated above—would feed on the rising nationalism of the younger people, stamping

* Characteristic of internal bureaucratic infighting and conflicts over domestic priorities was the following press report: "MITI, which stands for industrial development, maintains a very cautious attitude, only saying 'we have not yet been shown any plan concerning the character of the Environmental Agency.' International Trade and Industry Vice Minister Ojimi, however, hinted at his view that MITI's administrative functions may be hindered in some fields by the establishment of the Environmental Agency, saying as follows: 'Of MITI's bureaus and divisions, only the Public Nuisances Division of the Public Nuisances and Safety Bureau may be transferred to the new agency. After the establishment of the Environmental Agency, the private enterprises will have to deal with one more governmental organ. Also the problem of location of industries cannot be solved solely from the standpoint of preventing public nuisances'" (*Asahi Shimbun*, January 16, 1971).

the existing system with the label "made in U.S.A." and calling for a drastic reevaluation of social values.

Paradoxically—and this is a personal hunch disputed by many of my Japanese friends—Yukio Mishima could well become the symbol and the inspiration for this outlook. Though himself essentially a conservative nationalist, desperately desirous of a return to the true Japan of emperor worship, Mishima advocated—and dramatically personalized through his death—a rejection of the new "Americanized" Japan, with all its vulgarities, growing hedonism, lack of purpose, and crass concentration on the material. With a little bit of ideological surgery, he could even posthumously become a prophet of a new "people's Japan," which could seek to combine traditional patriotism with a new socialist austerity.

The other alternative would involve a more conservative response. The existing Establishment would adapt and co-opt the rising social concern as its own, and would make the growing ambivalence—not to speak of hostility—about the GNP part of its own program to recapture "the Japaneseness" of Japan, while still providing the masses with continued prosperity. Voices on that note are becoming more frequent; for example, Nobutane Kiuchi, a well-known conservative Japanese economist, has warned that today's Japan is a "distorted" Japan in that the emphasis on the GNP has been excessively motivated by the sense of insecurity and inferiority, by the desire to prove one's self by catching up with the industrially more advanced West. He thus advocates an "inward-looking" Japan, which would be concerned more with quality than with growth, somewhat more contemplative than primarily activist in its behavioral characteristics.

Even short of the above reorientation, it is already clear that the ruling party, and the business circles supporting and dominating it, are actively engaged in formulating programs designed to provide continued growth—at about 10 percent per annum—and paying much higher attention to the needs of what is sometimes called the social infrastructure. In addition to this, one may also expect from this side more emphasis on Japan's cultural uniqueness and national distinctiveness—the old Yamato spirit—as part of a broader program to make Japan into a uniquely Japanese domestic success story, thus combining conservative nationalism with progressive domesticism.*

SOCIAL METASTABILITY

Which of the two alternative responses will become dominant, or whether Japanese political life will become more polarized, will depend on other considerations discussed in the political part of this report, but it is clear already that Japanese society is entering a phase of complexity, with the post-war *gashin-shotan* mood a thing of the past. This phase of complexity is likely to be all the more unsettling because the uncertainty over goals and over the best means of pursuing them is likely to be accompanied by mounting cultural uncertainty, a kind of identity crisis postponed or, to use a psychoanalytic term, sublimated, during the recovery phase.

This cultural uncertainty—if the term "identity crisis" is too strong—involves a clash between Asianism and Westernism,

* The conservative response, it should be noted, has solid historical precedents. "Surely there is no more amazing instance in world history of the use of traditionalist means to radical ends than when the leaders of early Meiji masked the political changes which they had made with the label of an 'imperial restoration.' The effect was not only to give unprecedented policies the color of great antiquity, but also to make it appear that what was in fact an administration by relatively lowly placed new men proceeded instead from the most highly pedigreed and unquestionably legitimate of all possible sources. . . . In short, the overwhelmingly conservative associations of the imperial institution might be said to have been useful to the modernizers to the degree that they gave them freedom of action and placed a conservative face even on quite radical policies" (H. Webb, "The Development of an Orthodox Attitude Toward the Imperial Institution in the Nineteenth Century," in M. B. Jansen, ed., *Changing Japanese Attitudes Toward Modernization* [Princeton, N.J.: Princeton University Press, 1965], p. 188).

between Japaneseness and Americanization, between traditionalism and modernism (or social radicalism), between economism and hedonism. All of these tendencies are evident when dealing with the Japanese individually, and they affect Japanese political and international perspectives. It is striking how often the Japanese will emphasize their Asianness, either when speaking of their affinity for the Chinese or when recalling American discrimination against the yellow race, yet just as often the Japanese will boast that they are really the only Western-type society in a sea of Asian backwardness (and Japanese contempt for most other Asians, save the Chinese, is almost unmasked). Their deep and justifiable sense of pride in being Japanese has not prevented them from becoming "Americanized" in very many superficial but also in some deeper ways as well (e.g., a more democratic style among the younger generation), to a point where fears are now voiced that national traditions may be obliterated altogether and must therefore be deliberately promoted. Yet the desire to keep up with "modernization" is very strong, in part to prove Japanese superiority and in part out of insecurity, and that desire conflicts again with the traditional values.

Students of Japanese society have frequently noted that Japanese history has been punctuated by sudden—even dramatic—shifts.

> In her modern history Japan has seen three periods in which the country was very receptive to Western ideas. Each of the three periods followed immediately upon a great change in society: first, the Meiji Reform; second, the First World War; third, the Second World War. Each of them continued roughly for ten or fifteen years. Each was succeeded by a period of nationalism, in which the country was rather closed to Western ideas, ethical and political. In other words, there has been an alternating cycle of the periods of two different inclinations, toward the West and toward the Japanese traditions.*

* Shuichi Kato, "Japanese Writers and Modernization," in Jansen, *Changing Japanese Attitudes Toward Modernization,* p. 443–444. In a similar vein, Professor Reischauer has noted that "the Japanese have reflected these characteristics in the alternating periods in their history

What is striking about these shifts is the suddenness with which they come. This suddenness, however, should not be confused with impetuosity. Rather, it indicates another aspect of Japanese life worth noting. Though change occurs, every effort is made to mask it, to imply continuity with the past, to convey the impression that nothing much has changed. Just as emotion and anger are to be suppressed with full effort, so too continuity and tradition are seemingly asserted.[5] The foregoing seems to be in keeping with the

> dominant pattern in the Japanese mentality. It has a tendency to sidestep as far as possible any kind of confrontation. This, in turn, leads to the tendency to retain the existing stability with the least amount of modification and sacrifice of a thoroughgoing solution. It seems to avoid any form of rational compromise based on a selection from alternative possibilities.[6]

As a result of this predilection for abrupt change after considerable gestation, Japanese society can be said to be characterized by a kind of metastability, that is to say, a stability that appears to be extremely solid until all of a sudden a highly destabilizing chain reaction is set in motion by an unexpected input. The element of insecurity reinforces that stability, for the sense of insecurity makes stability a condition in which almost everyone has an interest; but once instability is set in motion, insecurity tends to intensify the instability. The conflict between modernization and traditionalism has a similar effect. To be sure, the Japanese society at this moment is quite stable, and the restraints

---

between abject humility towards outside civilizations and arrogant cultural independence and self-assertiveness. The hero of one period is the broad-minded leader who openly condemns Japanese failings and extolls the virtues of foreign cultures. Sooner or later he is replaced by a very different type of hero, who points out the corrupting influences of inferior foreign civilizations and calls for a return to native Japanese virtues. But, whichever type dominates a period, both are equally conscious of the contrast between Japan and the outside world" (*The United States and Japan,* 3rd ed. [Cambridge, Mass.: Harvard University Press, 1965], pp. 109–110).

on destabilizing factors are quite strong. The society has a resilient structure, and it is characterized by a very high degree of inner personal discipline. At the same time, however, this foreign observer leaves Japan with a feeling that serious strains are developing within Japanese society and that they will be reflected both in Japanese politics and economics.

2

Political Trends

FOR MORE THAN TWENTY YEARS, Japanese political life has been dominated by the Liberal Democratic party (LDP). That party's continuous control of government represents a unique success story among the world's democratic systems; no other major country has a matching record of political continuity.

In its essence, the reason for this success, and hence for the remarkable political stability of postwar Japan, is that the LDP was the only party capable of responding simultaneously to the basic concerns of the postwar Japanese electorate. These concerns involved, as a broad generalization, three key issues: economic recovery, alliance with the United States, and institutionalization of democracy.

Economic recovery was, obviously, a desperate need, one that could only be accomplished if national discipline was accompanied by a sound and effective mobilization of the nation's talents and resources, taking advantage of whatever immediate opportunity existed, without succumbing to remote doctrinal diversions. The reality of the American occupation and of Japan's economic dependence on American assistance dictated certain obvious conclusions.

The alliance with America followed similarly from the concrete situation. It was an imperative for both economic recovery and as a shield in the setting of the cold war. One of the most burning anxieties of the Japanese immediately after their defeat was that their country might be partitioned—like Germany—and that the Russians, whom the Japanese dislike intensely, might seize Hokkaido. Even after that immediate fear had waned, the cold war still created a sense of insecurity, which made a relatively close political relationship with the United States seem necessary and desirable to a majority of the Japanese, even though at times the opposition to this point of view attracted sizable minority support.

The institutionalization of democracy, in the wake of Japan's defeat by the United States, meant fundamentally one thing: the adoption of a political system modeled on the Western experience, with a large American input, even though adapted to the Japanese context (e.g., high affection for the Emperor). This meant defining democracy essentially in juridical or constitutional terms, with a high degree of stress on procedural safeguards, on the role of parties, and on political decentralization. For the Japanese, such a setup was also designed to offer guarantees against any return to prewar militarism.

Of the major postwar contenders for power, only the LDP could stand before the voters and convincingly argue that it could offer satisfaction on all three scores. None of the other parties could do so. The Socialists, who very briefly held the reins of power shortly after the defeat, were unconvincing on the economic question and later increasingly ambivalent about the relationship with the United States, although their democratic credentials were excellent. The Communists were suspect on all three scores.

NEW STRAINS

Today, the situation is becoming much less clear with regard to the predominant concerns of the voters. Many Japanese, especially the younger ones, tend to take the economic recovery for granted. Though prosperity is still a goal for many, economic growth is no longer a matter of survival. Similarly, an alliance with America, while apparently still supported by the majority, no longer seems to be a matter of life or death for the nation, while gradually rising nationalist sentiments make many Japanese feel that a basic review of that alliance, pointing toward a more even relationship, is becoming due. In addition, some others, those who desire a close relationship, are becoming apprehensive that America is no longer a reliable ally, while recent economic strains have made all groups more aware of conflict of interest between Japan and the United States. Finally, the question of democracy is no longer a lively issue for the majority, since democratic institutions appear to have worked well for the last two decades.

In addition to this waning preoccupation with the concerns listed above, the simultaneous satisfaction of which represented the success formula of the LDP, a growing but still minority portion of the Japanese is developing an altogether conflicting point of view. For some, especially the younger intelligentsia, economic growth is not a desirable social objective, since it contributes to lowering the intangibles involved in "the quality of life." There is a great deal of curiosity among this group with the American left-liberal concept of zero economic growth.

Politically more important, however, is the ambivalence felt by a large proportion of the urban electorate. It desires more prosperity but defines it increasingly in social as well as personal terms: better housing, social services and amenities, more welfare, more attention to dealing with the "public nuisances." It was these views that caused the major setbacks to the LDP in the 1971 urban elections and the corresponding gains of the JSP and the JCP.

The desirability of alliance with the United States is rejected also only by a minority. However, unlike the recent past, when it was rejected by a left doctrinal minority, there is now an increasing tendency among nonleftists—for example, even among the younger LDP leaders—to question the utility and acceptability of what is essentially still a highly asymmetrical relationship. While this point of view has not surfaced entirely, it is likely to be felt increasingly during the next several years—and of which more later.

Finally, the question of democracy for a minority that may be growing means more than political-constitutional safeguards; they argue that the time is now ripe for a social definition of democracy. In other words, more concentration on the deliberate promotion of social welfare and equality, a movement away from the capitalist model as the economic underpinning for a liberal democracy. The disillusionment of many Japanese with the United States, fed in part by old ideological biases lately reinforced by the Vietnamese war, and given real impetus by the seeming crisis within the United States, has helped to stimulate a more critical look by the Japanese at their own democracy. Added to this is the rise on the other extreme of small right-wing groupings, preaching a return to the traditional values of Japan of the early post-Meiji era, and finally of the Komeito party, the political arm of the militant Buddhist sect Soka Gakkai and a kind of Japanese Poujadism—neutralist in foreign policy, philosophically conservative, socially radical.

It is thus becoming much more difficult for the LDP to formulate a program capable of commanding majority support. The challenge that it faces today is how to identify correctly the basic concerns of the Japanese and to articulate in response the right prescriptions. This is not to say that some other party is in a better position to do so, even though it is a fact that a loose "anticoalition" appears to be gradually jelling. The anticoalition lacks structure and organization, and so far deliberate efforts to give it a formal expression have faltered because of the programmatic incompatibility of the different anti-groupings. At times, the left-wing JSP cooperates with the JCP; at other times, the JSP forges alliances with the more centrist Social Democratic party (SDP) and even the Komeito; while some of the more progressive LDP leaders have been speculating about an eventual coalition either with the SDP and/or the Komeito.

Thus the anti-Establishment, antibusiness, anti-GNP, anticapitalist forces are still disorganized, but together they are beginning to command an increasing share of the electorate. The extreme left combined (JSP and JCP) obtained 28 percent of the vote in the 1969 general elections; with the Komeito added, the total was 39 percent; with the SDP, it came to 46 percent, or almost as much as that obtained by the LDP, whose total percentage of the vote has been going steadily downward in every national election. In a word, the Japanese political picture is becoming both more fragmented and polarized, matching thereby the social patterns already noted.

Significant for the future is the decline of the LDP in the urban centers. The LDP has been traditionally stronger in the rural areas, and the electoral map has been drawn in such a manner that disproportionate representation has been enjoyed by the 17 percent of the population still engaged in agriculture. However, in the cities in the 1969 elections, the LDP got only about 39 percent of the vote, and in 1971 it was badly shaken in Tokyo and Osaka. To make matters worse, in the 1971 Upper House elections, in which the LDP normally should have done well, the opposition (involving in some cases local JSP-SDP-Komeito alliances) did surprisingly well in the rural areas.

Moreover, the extreme left appears to be renovating itself and adapting more quickly to the changing conditions of Japan than has the present LDP leadership. The JCP has been concentrating on improving its image: it has become more nationalistic in its pronouncements (even attempting to exploit the latent Japanese desire to obtain the return of the Hokkaido offshore islands, seized by the Soviet Union, indicating to the electorate that a leftist government in Japan would be more effective in pressing demands for the return of these islands, in spite of firm Soviet statements that the issue is closed); it has been concentrating more on the concrete problems of the Japanese urban voter and less on overall doctrinal goals; it has rejuvenated its leadership by placing in some key positions rather attractive and able young men; it has become more cooperative toward the other opposition parties.

Some leaders of the opposition hope that a strong left-wing coalition might emerge even as soon as in the near future, that is to say by 1975. Led either by the JCP or by the JSP, and occasionally cooperating with other opposition forces, it could become a formidable challenger, if not for power directly, then to the effective exercise of power. The Japanese political scene in that respect would then become similar to that of either France or Italy: the extreme left will be operating from a solid base of organized support, controlling from one-fourth to one-third of the electorate, and occasionally able, by exploiting specific crises or by expedient arrangements with other opposition groups, to foray in order to paralyze existing policies or even to make a serious grasp for power.

The key questions, accordingly, are what will happen to the LDP itself—or, in other words, how solid will the center-right be—and will Japan become like the France of the Fourth Republic, where a strong left is offset by a stronger center-right, or like Italy, where a strong left faces a relatively ineffective factionalized center? These are vital questions because of the LDP's critical role during the last twenty years. The very success of the LDP makes its future behavior the key to Japan's political future.

THE LDP'S CRISIS

At the moment, the LDP does not appear to be in very good shape. Its leadership seems to have become flabby, perhaps psychologically corrupted by success, old in age and even more in outlook, and subject to intensifying factional conflict. That conflict, to be sure, is not new, because the LDP has always been a somewhat loose coalition of personal factions, but the rivalry among these factions has lately been intensified by the likelihood that Prime Minister Eisaku Sato will retire by late 1972 at the very latest (and probably earlier) and by the growing realization, brought home by the recent electoral setbacks, that an era may be coming to an end.

The factional conflict at some point could even strain the formal organizational unity of the LDP itself. Some aspirants to leadership, impatient with the seeming conservatism of the present leaders, have talked of bolting and promoting instead a new coalition, resting on the more "progressive" LDP groupings and linked with the Komeito and SDP, while benefiting perhaps from the benevolent encouragement of the JSP and JCP, both desirous of breaking up the LDP. Though at the moment the prospects of such a breakup and of such an alternative coalition seem farfetched, it is certainly true that major divisive issues are beginning to reinforce the strong personal rivalries within the LDP, polarizing the conflicts on a left-right axis.

One issue is the already noted question of domestic policy, the matter of growth and quality, the imperative need to formulate a program that is simultaneously attractive to the urban electorate and to big business. A new issue is that of foreign policy, particularly as it pertains to China. In a way, China has become a symbolic as well as a real issue in Japanese politics. It is real in that obvious choices will have to be made soon, involving not only the United Nations but also such more immediately sensitive matters as Taiwan (where Japan has some major economic interests); it is symbolic in that the China question has become a litmus test for Japanese independence from the United States, for a new sense of national and perhaps even Asian self-assertiveness, and for a spirit of innovation within the LDP leadership. As a result, almost every aspiring LDP leader has found it necessary to make his position on China known, and even highly conservative leaders have found it necessary to indicate that they favor a change in Japanese-Chinese relations and that they would like to visit Peking.

The China issue could well become a trigger for a major intraparty split, pitting the presently established leadership—led by the prime minister and supported by his brother, former Prime Minister Nobusuke Kishi, and probably also by Foreign Minister Takeo Fukuda, Kishi's preferred successor to Sato, and probably Sato's as well—not only against such longer-term dissident leaders as Takeo Miki or Aiichiro Fujiyama (who has personally taken the lead in promoting semiofficial contact with China), but perhaps even against somewhat more "centrist" contenders for power, such as Masayoshi Ohira, Kakuei Tanaka, or Yasuhiro Nakasone.*

* A good example of attitudes toward China of the various competing LDP factions is to be found in the *Nihon Keizai Shimbun* (*The Japan Economic Journal*) of April 18, 1971. The article points out that Finance Minister Takeo Fukuda (appointed during the summer of 1971 to serve as foreign minister) for a long time avoided committing himself on the Chinese question, but, finally, in the spring of 1971, he began to shift toward a more flexible position, warning against excessive investments in Taiwan lest they irritate China. The story goes on to point out that Secretary General Kakuei Tanaka, though not directly indicating his own position, has gone out of his way to court those LDP leaders, like Aiichiro Fujiyama, who have become closely identified with a pro-Chinese position. Similarly, Masayoshi Ohira, a major contender for the prime ministership, has begun to disassociate himself from his previous position of supporting the Republic of China, indicating that Japan will have to be guided by the majority decision of the U.N. Takeo Miki, who previously contested Prime Minister Sato for the leadership of the party, has long advocated rapprochement between Tokyo and Peking and, according to the paper, is "seeking an opportunity where he himself can personally launch into this question, and he is gauging the timing when

Should that happen, a number of younger LDP aspirants, men in their early forties, may be tempted to support an upheaval in the established leadership. However, it is very important to note that these struggles—though focusing on large policy issues—are essentially personal and factional. Coalitions may thus shift suddenly, depending on personal ad hoc arrangements and divisive policy issues notwithstanding.

A brief word about the different leaders may therefore be in order. The prime minister, Eisaku Sato, is an extremely able and personable politician of considerable skill. He led the party to an unexpectedly assertive victory in 1969, and his capacity to project his personality is quite unusual, given the impersonal style of Japanese politics.

Among the other leaders, Ohira is a major dark horse, a shrewd and deliberate leader, somewhat Buddha-like in his manner, a former foreign minister likely to make a major bid for the leadership when Sato retires. He projects an air of deliberate determination. Foreign Minister Fukuda, who until the summer of 1971 served as finance minister, is of an extremely penetrating intellect, with occasional flashes of unexpected humor. Articulate and obviously able, he is a skilled technician, likely to provide the party with effective management, though it is less certain whether he can project a personal appeal.

Former Defense Minister Nakasone, who retired from the

---

he can become the leading force within the Party on the China question." Even more hawkish members, like Okinori Kaya, have come out in favor of Party leaders visiting China. *Nihon Keizai* concludes that "although there are differences and nuances, the general trend of the Party can be said to be moving at a fast pace toward the establishment of a set-up which would enable it to respond to changes in the future, based on the judgment that the time will come in the near future when it will be pressed to break the deadlock on the China question in some form or other. . . . Arguments within the Party, involving both hawk factions and dove faction members, are expected to become heated. There is no doubt at all that this will play the role of priming the water and that the changes in the undercurrent will develop into a big ground swell."

cabinet in the summer of 1971, is one of the younger contenders for power. Only fifty-three, he is likely to try to make a name for himself in domestic and foreign issues, having already established himself as an ambitious national leader of the Japanese Self-Defense Forces (SDF). He did much to energize these forces, to initiate the process of strategic thinking within the Japanese military hierarchy, and to give the personnel of the SDF a sense of professional pride. He may well now strive to identify himself either with domestic concerns, such as a more energetic program against public nuisances, or with a somewhat more nationally assertive foreign policy—for example, rapid movement toward China. At the same time he is clearly distrusted and disliked by many Japanese contemporaries, who see him as excessively ambitious and who are presumably fearful of his ability. Personable, intelligent, and self-assured, Nakasone strikes one as the type of leader who might be called upon in the event of a crisis but who in normal times is likely to generate too many enemies to be acceptable as a leader.

Tanaka, the party organizer appointed as minister of international trade and industry in the summer of 1971, is clearly a major contender for the leadership, should Fukuda be denied the spot. Like Nakasone only fifty-three and electorally appealing, he has been developing a highly personal style of political campaigning. However, although attractive and intelligent, he appears to be sensitive about his somewhat more limited education (he is not a member of the Tokyo University "club") and gives the impression of being uneasy with foreigners.

Among younger leaders, in their forties or less, mention should be made of Yohei Kono, son of a once-likely prime minister whose prospects were cut short by death. Kono, though only in his mid-thirties, has already developed a personal faction and is recognized as a potential leader in the future. Unlike some of the leaders in their sixties, Kono is himself attractive, articulate, and able to project a personal appeal. Impatient with the immobilism of the senior leadership, he is obviously casting both for a broader political education and for relevant issues.

In the interplay of the different factions, Ohira, for example, a man in his early sixties, former foreign minister and a recognized leader, could gain the leadership of the party and hence the prime ministership if supported by Tanaka, who by Japanese political standards is still quite young (not yet in his mid-fifties) and who for the last several years has been in charge of the party apparatus, especially if Ohira were to promise that Tanaka would succeed him. On the other hand, much the same ploy could be utilized by Fukuda to gain Tanaka's support, with Fukuda's more advanced age serving as a more credible guarantee to Tanaka that Fukuda's tenure in office would not be too long. Nakasone, Tanaka's contemporary and rival, presumably would play a similar game, but his factional base is much smaller. An "outsider" to this game might be Miki, who already once contested Sato and did better than observers expected. He would base his campaign, as already noted, on the China issue. In general, it would seem probable that if Sato steps down soon, Fukuda would inherit his post; if he delays, it could be either Ohira or even, though his age clearly works against him, Tanaka, although the electoral setbacks in the summer of 1971 may well rebound against him.

In addition to personalities, a more basic factor in these factional conflicts, especially on the less tangible level of personal-psychological compatibility and empathy, involves generational differences. The present LDP leadership is quite old; it is held by a group of former financial bureaucrats whom the MacArthur purge of Japanese political and business leaders left unscathed and who quickly filled the political vacuum thereby created. These men have dominated Japanese political life for almost twenty years. As a result, men like Tanaka or Nakasone are considered to be young because they are almost in their mid-fifties. This leaves way behind some of the ambitious and increasingly impatient LDP aspirants who are only in their early forties and who, in large measure because of frustration and impatience, are then driven to embrace a more extremist position as a way of making a name for themselves. Some have hence openly advocated that Japan become a nuclear power, others have been plunging into the China issue, especially since the press has been playing it up, and still others have been tempted to identify themselves with such domestic causes as the struggle against public nuisances, even at the expense of alienating some of the key financial groups on which the LDP traditionally has relied. It could happen that an ambitious leader like Nakasone—if not effectively co-opted by his elders—will become the standard-bearer of the LDP's Young Turks.

In any case, it is very likely that the present LDP leadership—essentially conservative in outlook, cautious in its policies, not very imaginative in its thinking—will, in the near future, undergo a very basic change. At most, Fukuda or even Ohira will be transitional leaders, either paving the way for a somewhat different orientation and political style or presiding over the further decline of the LDP. Pressures for the party to redefine its stand on China, to focus energetically on rising domestic problems (notably inflation, taxation, housing, and public nuisances), and somehow to be responsive to the still undefined but perceptively spreading sense of national self-assertiveness are rising, and any would-be leader will have to find a satisfactory formula embracing all three—much as his predecessors did in the first twenty postwar years to another set of basic domestic concerns.

TOWARD PERSONALIST POLITICS

All of this will be taking place in the setting of a striking change in the Japanese political style, a change bound to affect very fundamentally the character of the Japanese political game. As already noted, one of the most notable features of Japanese politics is the role of personal cliques or factions within parties, especially within the dominant LDP. It is through the interaction of the various cliques that policy and personal choices are made, and it is through these factions that political funding is arranged. It is also through a gradually emerging consensus that the leader is chosen, and the leader is leader because his personal faction, in alliance with several others, is able to manipulate the political balance. Moreover, given the highly indirect and rather covert process of inner bargaining that is involved, the leader that emerges is rarely characterized by what in the West would be considered charismatic qualities. (Mr. Sato's rather attractive personality is a novelty, and his ability to project himself may have something to do with the unprecedented length of his tenure.) Rather, he tends to be a compromise choice, equal among equals, not a man who would stand out and be viewed by the Japanese electorate as a national leader.*

I believe that the pattern of clique politics is beginning to change, and that Japanese politics will be undergoing—are, in fact, already undergoing—a shift toward a more personalized style of politics. Prime Minister Sato himself may be a symptom of this change, and the opposition parties have likewise been gravitating in the direction of more personalized politics (their victory, for example, in the Tokyo gubernatorial race is largely due to the more attractive image of the opposition candidate, and the Communist party has already chosen as a leader an attractive thirty-nine-year-old intellectual, something most unusual in Japanese politics). The younger LDP leaders, like Nakasone or

* In that sense, Japanese politics display some characteristics reminiscent of British politics in the pre-Wilson era (excepting the crisis circumstances of Churchillian governance). The prime minister was usually a compromise choice, while the electorate tended to vote more on the basis of local candidates or party preferences than because of the personal appeal of the prime minister. Much of that has changed with the advent of the TV age, and Heath's victory in 1970 was even credited by many to his effective use of television, especially in the competitive appearance with then-Prime Minister Wilson.

Tanaka, have been fascinated by the use of television by American leaders, especially Kennedy, and they have eagerly absorbed the lessons of that experience.*

More important than the subjective interest of would-be leaders is the fact that television has become a key instrument of mass communication in Japan and that political leaders have no choice but to avail themselves of it. This inherently places a certain premium on personality, and makes the effective use of mass media (including newspapers) a central vehicle for personal political success.† Moreover, it appears that the effective projection of personality has a larger impact on women‡ and on the younger voters, less tied to established party loyalties and more inclined to make ad hoc judgments, either on the basis of existing circumstances or on personal empathy. Since both groups are becoming increasingly important in Japanese politics, it is likely that they will strengthen the trend toward personalized politics.

The result—likely to become more visible during the next several years—will be a more direct and personal relationship between the leader and the voters and will mean—once the choice of leader is made, assuming that the party is successful in choosing an attractive leader—a corresponding, though gradual, decline in the importance of cliques, for the direct relationship with the voters will increasingly tend to free the leader from dependence on clique support. The elevation in national importance of

* When I mentioned to one leading Japanese contender that appearance, coolness, and sincerity were the three principal assets of effective TV campaigners, he took out a notebook and, asking me to repeat the above, wrote them down. Fortunately for him, the first—which is not usually subject to control—is in his favor, the second is quite characteristic of him, while the third quality he might be able to feign!

† Public opinion polls indicate that voters, asked to indicate "the most helpful reference in choosing a candidate," identified newspapers, television, and radio more than any other source (41 percent as compared with the next influence, family discussions, which obtained 19 percent) (*Mainichi Shimbun,* December 16, 1969).

‡ The previously cited polls indicate that the choice of women, more so than men, is based on their judgment of the person, rather than on the party involved.

the political leader in turn will involve a gradual but important move toward a "presidential" style, in both electoral campaigns and government, of the sort that the British and French have adopted in the wake of the American experience.

Such a development will mean, finally, a departure from the established pattern of Japanese political culture. The elevation of a single *personality* (not only of an impersonal person, like the Emperor of old, but of personality, of a personal image) as the dominant political figure will be a break with the deeply ingrained tradition of government by collective, impersonal decision-making, by almost invisible consensus, by self-effacing chairmen of almost co-equal factional chieftains.

If carried too far—and, initially at least, Japanese traditions and the continued importance of cliques for political funding will stand in the way of it being carried too far—this could also introduce a personally demagogic style into Japanese politics. Until now, the Japanese have not been exposed on a national scale to politically significant personal demagogy. Tojo was not a demagogue like Mussolini or Hitler, and Japanese democratic politicians have been more reminiscent of Coolidge or Hoover than of Kennedy or Reagan. Personalist politics carry with them the latent danger of demagogy, though—as noted—the tradition of personal restraint and self-effacement will initially work against such a development. Nonetheless, the danger could become quite real, particularly if this emergence of personalist politics were to be coupled with a national crisis of some sort.

PRELIMINARY PROGNOSIS

Given all the foregoing considerations, what kind of a *preliminary* political prognosis is reasonable for the next several years? The opposition, although gaining in support, still seems too weak to become sufficiently powerful by mid-decade to assume political power. The Komeito, though led by rather energetic and dedicated younger men,* seems to have capitalized on the doctrinaire excesses of the JSP and to reflect the interests of a special class, the lower middle class, of Japanese. Its potential for further growth is questionable. The JSP and the JCP appeal basically to the same constituencies: to the intellectuals, including some of the students of voting age; to the marginal members of the creative-artistic community; to the more vulnerable lower-income urban dwellers; and lately to some of the disaffected farmers, uneasy over the LDP's agricultural support policies. Potentially, these groupings—especially if a coalition with the Komeito could be contrived—could represent a majority of the Japanese electorate.

However, whether the opposition parties can coalesce into such a coalition is very dubious. Here the question of traditional behavior again comes into the picture. Given rather narrow party or group loyalties, and given the habit of effective work primarily within one's own grouping, it is likely to prove very difficult for Japanese politicians of differing ideological persuasions to make the necessary compromises for an enduring coalition.† Ad hoc

* I met with a number of the senior Komeito leaders and I was impressed by their sincerity, their energy, and their relative youthfulness. They struck me very much as men who know what they want and are unencumbered by the past, and hence are able to introduce new techniques and style into Japanese politics. For example, the Komeito leadership is relying on the use of computers to develop an alternative concept to GNP, one stressing more personal happiness and collective welfare. At the same time, they gave me the impression of being relatively unsophisticated, in some respects simplistic in their doctrines, rather reminiscent of middle-class American Rotarians or senior Boy Scouts.

† Japanese sociologist Nakane suggests that "for a variety of reasons, it is difficult for a Japanese to establish operational contractual personal relations." She notes that Japanese find it very difficult to establish a relationship outside of the parties within which they have become accustomed to work and that "each party tends to monopolize his partner's loyalty, though it may be utterly unnecessary for the completion of the work." She goes on to suggest that "if a man is invited to join a new group he may try his best, as a mother hen with her brood, to take along his whole entourage to the new group; he may still hold loyalty to his former group. These factors intimately affect functioning

arrangements, focused on specific electoral contests and therefore also confined in time, might achieve some successes against the LDP, but that is not the same thing as successfully cooperating in forming and running a stable government. Added to these considerations are the obvious doctrinal differences still dividing the opposition parties.

More likely, therefore, is an effort by the LDP to preempt and co-opt the programs of the opposition, to refocus its policies from rapid growth to something more generally concerned with the "quality of life," and to retain control of the government on that basis. Ambitious national goals for domestic improvement have already been formulated, and the LDP is bound to remain in a better position to solicit business support and cooperation for their implementation. (The foreign equivalent of this orientation might be a somewhat more independent policy, less inclined to dovetail in most respects with the United States, on which more later.)

However, though the LDP is likely to remain the dominant political force, it will probably become less cohesive, more subject to internal splits. A partial coalition with outside forces may—as already noted—tempt some of its leaders, and a coalition with the Komeito or with the SDP or with both would perhaps involve fewer personal strains and doctrinal incompatibilities than an attempt to organize a corresponding coalition among the opposition parties. Nonetheless, it, too, would run into the inherent difficulty of promoting effective cooperation outside of familiar group frameworks.

The likely pattern, therefore, is something between that of Italy and of France. The left is not likely to become quite as cohesive as either the French Communist party or the Italian

---

of the new group. Because loyalty is emotional, it does not lend itself to division" (Chie Nakane, *Japanese Society* [London: Weidenfeld and Nicolson, 1970], p. 80). These considerations would apply directly to the problem of an enduring coalition.

Communist party, with each of them by itself commanding about one-fourth of the French or the Italian electorate; the Japanese left, though gaining in strength, will lack organizational unity, even though the JCP might emerge in it as the vital energizing force. At the same time, the Japanese center-right is likely to remain more cohesive than that of Italy, but perhaps not quite as organizationally and personally directed as the post–de Gaulle centrist-right in France, especially given the presidential-type constitution of the Fourth Republic. It will take time for the LDP to develop and acknowledge a dominant personal leader. Until then, intensifying factional conflict, reinforced by policy dilemmas, is likely to dilute its cohesion and very severely test its unity. A phase of political confusion, even of chaotic cabinet instability, is a real possibility for the mid-seventies.

The great unknown in all of this is the extent of popular commitment to democracy itself. Democracy was imposed on Japan from outside, though it does appear to have been genuinely accepted. That acceptance, however, was reinforced by two conditions, one external, one internal. Externally, the enormous prestige of the United States strengthened the appeal of Western democracy to many Japanese. A crisis of Western democratic institutions could have the effect of tarnishing that appeal for the Japanese, especially if institutional malfunctions began to appear in Japan itself. The internal condition was that of economic recovery. Democracy took root while Japan was recovering and becoming more prosperous. How deep the Japanese commitment to democracy will prove itself, especially should economic difficulties become acute, no one can say with certainty, but economic well-being is certainly a key factor in reducing political tension and in moderating tendencies toward political polarization. That is why a more confident political prognosis must also take into account Japan's economic prospects.

3

Economic Prospects

JAPANESE ECONOMIC DEVELOPMENT ITSELF is so very much affected by noneconomic considerations, both domestic and external, that purely economic judgments tend to be one-sided. The scale of Japanese economic success is now well known—the Japanese lead the world in shipbuilding, in electronic production (radios, cameras, and transistorized television sets), motorcycles, and a variety of other fields; they are second to the United States in such areas as computers, rayon, aluminum, steel, and so forth—and some Japanese have become almost intoxicated by it. Late in the sixties and even in 1970, one would hear many Japanese repeat, uncritically and with pride, foreign projections indicating that by the year 2000 Japan would be the number one economic power and that the twenty-first century will be a Japanese century.*

However, the phase of Japanese boasting about all this did not last long. By 1971, the boast had come to an abrupt end—not

* Similarly, present projections of the growth rate of my seven-year-old son indicate that by the year 2000 he will be thirty-five feet tall!

that growth is no longer desired or that Japanese economic successes are no longer a source of pride, but largely because the Japanese are becoming increasingly aware that their own growth creates domestic and international difficulties. There is thus also an element of deliberate disingenuousness in the quick toning down of GNP-boasting, partially due to the realization that it is stimulating foreign fears, envy, and stiffer competition. Accordingly, some self-serving growth utility is involved in the current Japanese emphasis on their difficulties.

However, it is an obvious fact that Japanese economic well-being is central to Japan's social and political stability. Moreover, it is much the point of departure for a major international role—of whatever character—to which many patriotic Japanese aspire. Most Japanese still feel that high rates of growth are the foundation of Japan's prosperity and power.

There is no doubt that a significant slowdown would make both domestic and external choices sharper, would intensify social cleavages and political tensions. A major slowdown would make more acute the dilemmas already generated by the high rates of growth in the past decade, thereby posing a paradox: the problems created by high rates of growth, while in some respects made still worse by continued high rates, can only be tackled effectively in the setting of continued relatively high rates.

Accordingly, in spite of the criticisms voiced with increasing frequency, the predominant Japanese inclination is to maintain the momentum of rapid growth, though trying to stabilize it at roughly 10 to 11 percent per annum, a rate somewhat lower than the rates of 12 percent, 13 percent, or even 15 percent attained in the latter parts of the decade of the sixties. The somewhat lower rate—but one still extraordinarily impressive, given the size and complexity of Japan's economy—is viewed by Japanese economic leaders (leaving aside their desire, which doubtless is quite strong, simply to become number one) as striking the proper balance between the need to maximize Japan's trading position, to obtain and secure a wider access to raw materials, to maintain domestic social-political stability, and to obtain the necessary margins for dealing with the already noted domestic inadequacies, yet without generating an inflationary spiral, which still higher rates would set in uncontrollable motion. The crucial question, therefore, is whether such higher rates of growth can be maintained during this decade, at a time when, as we have seen, a number of political-social issues will be becoming more complex.

CAUSES OF SUCCESS

Any answer must, by its very nature, be speculative, but any attempt at an answer must take into account the comprehensive causes for Japan's recent successes. These successes have been the by-product of Japanese ingenuity and energy, as well as of specific internal and external circumstances. On the basis of conversations with business figures and economists, and on the basis of available literature on Japanese economic development, I drew up a list of some twenty factors that cumulatively contributed to Japan's economic success. A brief comment follows each, and then their relative importance is evaluated and their continued validity assessed:

1. An abundant and increasingly well-educated labor force. Cheap labor was available because of the extremely depressed postwar state of living and because of migration from rural to urban areas; literacy and excellent lower-level education, available since at least the Meiji period, meant that this labor force was easily adaptable to the industrial process.

2. High labor motivation and employment loyalty. The sense of self-discipline, in part traditional, in part stimulated by the postwar spirit of self-denial, as well as intense motivation and loyalty to employing companies, which in turn assumed broad responsibility not only for wages but for housing and other amenities, made for high performance and group cohesion.

3. Low wages. The first two factors above made it possible

to maintain for a long time an extraordinarily low level of remuneration by comparable industrial—not only Asian—standards.

4. High personal savings. The tradition of very high personal savings—much higher than in other corresponding industrial societies, the Japanese rate being approximately 20 percent while in other major countries the range was from 6 to 13 percent—gave Japanese banks a strong economic position and provided needed funds for capital investment.

5. Social stability. The postwar period has been characterized by a high degree of political continuity and, despite occasional strikes and—at one point—even a high degree of Communist penetration of trade unions, by a relative absence of major and sustained labor strife.

6. Increasing domestic consumption. The high rate of personal savings notwithstanding, domestic demand for consumer items has been rising steadily, until now benefiting from a growing and uncritical consumption orientation, thereby creating an expanding and dominant domestic market for Japanese industry.

7. The availability of seaport and coastal industrial sites. The rapid reconstruction of war-devastated ports and the eagerness of other communities to get into the act meant that expanding industry could take advantage of relatively easily available industrial sites, accessible by cheap maritime transportation.

8. Youthful and vigorous economic elite. The postwar economic takeoff followed shortly on the heels of the purge of the Japanese prewar and wartime leadership, with the result that a new and relatively youthful economic leadership, dominated by men in their late forties and early fifties, emerged, and has enjoyed an unprecedented twenty years of stable tenure.

9. Constructive role of government. At the same time, the postwar government, staffed largely by people of the same generation and even professional background as the new business elite, adopted a protective and highly cooperative relationship with the business community, with such key governmental organs as

the Finance Ministry and the Ministry of International Trade and Industry assuming an overall guiding role, defining—more through consultation than through centralized direction—basic choices and priorities and emphasizing longer-range planning, in order to gain for Japan the maximum benefits from economic leapfrogging.

10. Corporate cooperation. Though the Japanese cartels were broken up, the tradition of cooperative arrangements was not uprooted. The need to pull together during the recovery phase was overwhelming, while the relatively cohesive character of the Japanese political-economic elite automatically induced a rather accommodating pattern of corporate behavior, permitting a more effective division of effort and allocation of resources.

11. Heavy equipment investment. With choices more clearly defined, Japanese business undertook a policy of extremely high-level investment in modern equipment, involving on the average during the fifties and sixties more than 30 percent of the GNP in fixed capital formation, much more than the corresponding 17 percent in the United States or even the 24 percent in the similarly recovering and rapidly growing West German economy.

12. Banking structure. Japanese banks, backed by a social propensity toward high savings, played a key role in financing enterprises, in balancing the flow of capital, and in forestalling major business failures.

13. Stiff exchange controls. These provided the Japanese economy with the needed shield against speculation, protected the yen and the development of promising industries, and avoided the outflow of needed Japanese capital and the internal take-over of Japanese industries by foreign interests.

14. The low value of the yen. This low value provided the Japanese exports with a competitive advantage that became more and more marked as the Japanese economy began to export more and more technology- and science-intensive products.

15. Low defense expenditures. For a number of years about nil, and lately under 1 percent of the GNP, low defense expenditures meant that the Japanese industry, although perhaps not benefiting from military research and development spinoff, could concentrate its resources in areas offering the greatest competitive payoff.

16. U.S. economic paternalism. Motivated by the political desire to promote a strong Japan as a counterweight to Communist China, the United States promoted, in the General Agreement on Tariffs and Trade (GATT) and elsewhere, the recovery of the Japanese economy, in spite of Japanese restrictions on foreign imports and investments.

17. Free trade context. The above was especially beneficial to Japan, for the postwar era during the fifties and sixties was dominated by the U.S.-propagated atmosphere of free trade, thereby creating markets, especially in America itself, for Japanese exports.

18. Availability of foreign technology. The deliberate allocation of longer-range priorities and the exploitation of the advantageous free-trade situation enabled Japanese industry to undertake a broad program of importing and rapidly adapting to its needs advanced foreign technology, with striking successes in such areas as electronics, shipbuilding, steel, automobiles, and textiles, without the high costs involved in indigenous research and experimentation.

19. Raw materials. The global postwar development boom opened to the Japanese broad opportunities for access to raw materials, ranging from Australia, Peru, and Chile to India and the Middle East.

20. Local wars and American purchases. Both the Korean and the Vietnamese wars stimulated urgent American purchases in Japan and the rapid development of these Japanese industrial sectors of tactical and strategic importance to the American war effort. More broadly, the Korean War made the Americans more

anxious to see the speedy recovery of the Japanese industrial potential and accelerated the flow into Japan of American capital designed to advance that objective.

The above list, doubtless, could be somewhat expanded or condensed, depending on how the different factors are defined, but it represents, cumulatively, the variety of causes that permitted Japanese energy and ingenuity to attain such an impressive success. Before evaluating the list to determine how and to what extent conditions have now changed, it will be useful to review briefly some of the emerging problems confronting the Japanese economy. Some of them have already been mentioned in our social and political comments, but their relevance to the economic picture should be restated.

ECONOMIC CLOUDS

That a basic change in Japanese domestic values is taking place has already been noted. There is a growing uneasiness with the excessive preoccupation with the material aspects of life; there is a sudden boom in Japanese culture, renewed interest in preserving what remains of the past. The economic-political elite itself is affected by this change, its basic commitment to continued high growth notwithstanding. Moreover, there is an emerging consensus that a massive effort to improve the way the Japanese live and to give Japanese society a culturally satisfying identity of its own, not submerged in the characterless global industrial culture, is a central national imperative.*

* I was much impressed in the course of my conversations with top executives by the extent to which they expressed views along these lines, emphasizing the need for the business community to develop wider, more socially and culturally oriented goals. There was also much stress on the need to forecast the consequences of business or technological initiatives, with some of them even speculating that wealth could become a negative value, replaced by a quest for economic security and cultural satisfaction. Doubtless, a lot of that is fashionable rhetoric, but changes in rhetoric usually precede changes in more basic values. Moreover, American influence is very relevant here.

Accordingly, Japanese resources will have to be committed on an ever-increasing scale either to redirect or to disperse the so-far unchecked urbanization, to provide—on a massive scale—new housing, to improve woefully lacking sanitation, to cope with the imbalance between motorization and available roads, to reduce and eventually to eliminate pollution, to develop an effective and just social welfare system (including health and old-age care),* to deal with the inequalities in remuneration, and to develop a modern and socially, as well as economically, relevant educational system, especially on the upper levels.

Concern with these matters is beginning to move beyond the phase of rhetoric, though the consequences of any basic shift in priorities are yet to be felt or even to be fully anticipated. Ambitious plans for a future Japan, combining prosperity with quality, have been unveiled by all political parties. The most important of these, for obvious reasons, has been the official one, already unveiled in May 1969, which calls for a comprehensive regional reorganization of Japanese society, for demographic and economic decentralization, for more conservation, for a deliberate national policy of land utilization, for new transportation networks, for a national housing policy, designed both to alleviate existing congestion and to eventually reduce the demographic overconcentration in a few key metropolitan centers. Subsequent official proposals have elaborated on the above in greater detail "based on the realization that the day is over when Japan can be content with the mere growth of the gross national product and that an industrial policy attending to the 'heart' is now needed."† Noteworthy is the fact that the fulfillment of the

* Japanese social security, as a percentage of national income, is somewhat lower than that of the United States, and between two and three times lower than in the more advanced West European industrial societies.

† *Asahi Evening News,* May 19, 1971. These plans involve much stress both on ecological goals and on improvements in education, in addition to the items already mentioned.

targets set depends on a growth rate of 10 percent per annum in real terms during the 1970s.

What the actual costs of the above will be, and how the pursuit of socially desirable but in some cases economically non-profitable goals may affect the economy's overall growth rate is difficult even for economists to predict. One student of Japanese economics, in his study of the likely prospects for the Japanese economy, cites calculations of the Japanese Economic Planning Agency to the effect that "a 5% increase in fiscal expenditures —with the tax burden unchanged and a 0.6% rise in interest rates—might reduce the real growth rate by 3% per year."[1]

Also to be taken into account is the problem of labor supply and wage levels. Japan has been remarkably successful in checking the demographic explosion—in fact, some Japanese feel that they have been too successful. As a result, labor is already now in short supply, and the problem will become more acute during the next several years. The number of eighteen-year-old youths entering the labor market in 1966 was 1,240,000; it is expected that in 1974 the figure will be 770,000. In 1970–71, the Labor Ministry estimated the current shortage of skilled labor at 1,820,000 persons,[2] while MITI officials told me that they expect female employment to decline from its level of 50.6 percent in 1970 to 45 percent by 1980 (because of longer schooling and higher prosperity).

At the same time, for cultural-political reasons (involving both a high degree of insular exclusiveness as well as political prudence), the Japanese are determined to avoid the social complications involved in the importation of foreign labor. Though cheap labor could be easily had from neighboring sources of supply (particularly Korea and Hong Kong), the initial and probably enduring Japanese reaction is to shudder with horror at the prospect of several hundred thousand foreigners having to be assimilated into the Japanese economy and society. Indeed, Japanese sensitivity toward foreigners is a very major factor in the Japanese unwillingness to import foreign labor. Moreover, there are specific problems as well: most Japanese tend to look down on the Koreans, whom they consider to be untrustworthy and somehow inferior; at the same time, they admire the Chinese. Neither group, therefore, appears to be a suitable candidate for the menial but somewhat intimate relationship pertaining to imported labor.

The short labor supply has already had one very significant effect: an accelerating upward spiral in wage demands. During the 1960s wages rose on the average at about 11.5 percent, with a 13.6 percent rise in 1968, 15.6 percent in 1969, and 18 percent in 1970. Though this rate of increase may not continue indefinitely, it does mean that Japanese labor costs are losing some of their competitive advantage, while the competition for labor within Japan has pushed upward existing wages, particularly of skilled younger workers, to the disadvantage of the seniority system, the potential effect of which is to undermine one of the foundations for employment loyalty.

Labor unions are bound to exploit this situation by demanding better conditions and higher wages. In a comprehensive "White Paper on Wages for 1971," put out by the General Council of Trade Unions of Japan (SOHYO), a large number of grievances were outlined, especially in comparison to the welfare arrangements and social conditions prevailing in other advanced countries, particularly western Europe (the fact of the comparison itself underlines the enormous progress that Japan has already made). Significantly, not only were wage and welfare improvements demanded, but opposition was registered to "all enterprise rationalization programs,"[3] posing the specter (so familiar already to some sectors of the American economy) of labor opposition to technologically oriented improvements in industrial productivity.

In a word, the shortage of labor is likely to have several complicating consequences: it will push wages up, thereby complicating the efforts to control inflation; it will create labor unrest; and it will stimulate a decline in the loyalty of labor to their companies.

Japan may also encounter increasing difficulties in her access to raw materials. Though Japanese foreign trade involves a relatively small proportion of the GNP—actually smaller than before World War II—Japanese dependence on raw materials means that any major interference with their flow, and therefore also in Japanese trade, would before long have calamitous domestic consequences. Japanese domestic natural resources—barring some unexpected discoveries—are approaching exhaustion, and Japanese dependence on foreign sources is steadily increasing; given the ambitious goal of an average 10 percent per annum economic growth (not to speak of even higher projections popularized by some foreign forecasters), these needs are likely to grow dramatically. Japanese sources estimate that Japanese dependence on imports of copper is likely to grow from the present level of approximately 75 percent to over 90 percent by 1975; in lead, to nearly 60 percent; in iron ore from 85 percent to about 90 percent; in coal from under 75 percent to over 85 percent; in natural gas, it is likely to grow from a relatively low level presently to approximately 75 percent; and it is likely to remain at 100 percent in aluminum, nickel, oil, and uranium. Moreover, in terms of volume, actual needs will almost double.

Yet it is far from certain that access to these supplies will be readily available or that their costs will not rise perceptibly, given social and political instability in some areas of supply, mounting international competition, and rising resentment in some key areas (e.g., Indonesia or Australia) over Japanese investment efforts designed to assure Japan firm control of the needed supplies. The rise in the international price of oil, negotiated under some duress between the oil countries and the major oil companies in early 1971, immediately generated a great deal of Japanese anxiety and did involve, shortly thereafter, higher domestic prices of fuel in Japan. The Japanese fuel costs (excluding higher needs) will rise from $2.5 billion in 1970 to $4 billion in 1975 under the new price system. In all probability, the costs will be actually higher, given both rising needs and the likelihood of further price increases.

There is also still considerable uncertainty surrounding the future position of the yen. The Japanese have argued that their position should not be compared to that of the German mark; unlike the German case, Japanese domestic reserves are still relatively low, while Japanese foreign exchange controls are high. This means that the Japanese are not in as strong a position as the West Germans and that the opportunities for foreign speculation are much more limited. Their arguments notwithstanding—and it is clear that they were motivated almost entirely by self-interest—international pressure set in motion by the drastic financial measures adopted by the Nixon administration in August 1971 finally compelled the Japanese to free-float the yen, despite quite strong resistance and political pledges to the contrary.

As a result, the wide competitive advantage that Japanese goods have enjoyed on the international market, especially in the United States, is likely to be narrowed.* Protectionist tenden-

* MITI calculations show that an upward revaluation of 5 percent of the yen will work to reduce the export values of twenty-one major commodities by more than 10 percent for thirteen items, including the sharpest dip of 18.7 percent for electronic calculators:

	% *Decrease*		% *Decrease*
Iron and steel	13.39	Synthetic yarns	7.65
Shipbuilding	7.65	Made-up textile goods	11.88
Autos	11.13	Prime movers	9.61
Optical machines	11.88	Footwear	17.17
Radios	14.90	Textile machinery	8.11
Synthetic fabrics	8.86	Heavy electric machinery	10.37
Apparel	14.15	Porcelain	16.41
Tape recorders	16.41	Sewing machines	14.15
Organic chemicals	8.86	Electronic desk-top calculators	18.68
TV sets	17.92		
Cotton fabrics	9.62		
Motorcycles	7.35		

Nihon Keizai Shimbun, July 13, 1971.

cies will mean that the Japanese will be forced to import more foreign goods (rather than raw materials) or their own exports will suffer. The textile crisis with the United States was an augury of things to follow; an automobile crisis could be next. West Europe for some time has been more protectionist toward Japanese goods, and enlargement of the Common Market is not viewed by Japanese businessmen as necessarily enhancing their export opportunities.

Moreover, given the increasing sophistication of the Japanese industry and the increasing dependency of Japanese exports on technology- and science-intensive products, much more of an effort will have to be made to promote indigenous research and development. As often noted, until now the Japanese have benefited from a quick, very ingenious, but relatively inexpensive adaptation of the latest foreign technology to their own industrial processes, which—since they were being rebuilt almost from scratch—then became extremely advanced. That phase is rapidly ending. All Japanese businessmen I talked to have stressed the necessity of Japan's quickly developing its own research and development (R & D) personnel, laboratories, and think-tanks (the latter in particular are proliferating and have become a kind of industrial status symbol; every major company has to have one of its own). Present Japanese plans call for an R & D effort by 1980 roughly comparable to the level of the European Economic Community (EEC) and the Soviet Union.

Given Japanese skill and energy, these plans are likely to be fulfilled. But they will prove, first of all, more costly than the adaptation of foreign research to Japanese needs. The present status of Japanese higher education is also such that a broadly gauged effort to improve Japanese institutes of technology and scientific training will have to be made if success is to be attained. More important still—and more difficult and even unpredictable —is the question of the suitability of the present Japanese structure and outlook to highly innovative and creative R & D.

American experience, at least, shows that a fair amount of decentralization, willingness to run high risks, toleration of the unorthodox, and delegation of a great deal of authority and leeway to young scientists and managers is a precondition for creative R & D. It is not certain that this approach needs to be duplicated by the Japanese to insure success, but it is possible that their present structure, with its reliance on seniority and internal patterns of accommodation, may not prove as suitable for creative indigenous R & D as for adaptive reliance on foreign R & D.

DECISION-MAKING

This brings us to some observations on the vaunted style of Japanese decision-making and its bearing on Japanese economic prospects. That style of decision-making, involving essentially a highly informal pattern of gradually shaping collective consensus and avoiding explicit individual advocacy, seems to be deeply rooted in Japanese tradition. Resting on the concept of *ringisei,* which literally means "a system of reverential inquiry about the superior's intentions,"* the Japanese decision-making process is a study in prudence, circumspection, and collective responsibility. According to Peter Drucker's suggestive analysis, entitled "What We Can Learn From Japanese Management,"[4] this process is one of the key reasons for Japanese economic success. It enables the Japanese management to define key questions accurately and "it makes for very effective decisions."

* "It is an archaic term that is scarcely comprehensible to many postwar Japanese. Yet it is commonly used in academic and professional circles to describe a method of decision-making that has been extensively employed in Japanese governmental and private agencies since the early days of the Meiji era (1868–1912). . . . One should be aware of the fact that it is far more than an administrative technique. *Ringisei* actually is a fundamental characteristic of Japanese administrative behavior, organization, and management" (Kiyoaki Tsuji, "Decision-Making in the Japanese Government: A Study of Ringisei," in Robert E. Ward, ed., *Political Development in Modern Japan* [Princeton, N.J.: Princeton University Press, 1968], pp. 457–58). Tsuji goes on to describe in detail the actual administrative process involved.

My own impressions are somewhat different. No doubt that this system has worked well so far, but it has worked well while other things have also worked well. In other words, we really do not know how such a system would work in conditions of stress and crisis. We do know, however, that during World War II a comparable decision-making process in the Japanese government worked extremely badly; it proved simply impossible for the decision-makers to focus *quickly* on unpleasant choices, everyone's inclination simply being, with prudence and circumspection, to quietly pass the buck. The emphasis on group harmony thus tends to paralyze the group, making it immobile or tardy when confronted with difficult or unexpected choices.*

As a perceptive Japanese sociologist has noted, "the urge towards maximum consultation, regardless of the nature and size of a group, frequently results in interminably long meetings, dragged out in the name of 'democracy.' Japan is today the land of meetings, and it is far from difficult to find a man who spends more time at meetings than at his desk."[5] Moreover, there is a strong inclination in such a setting to avoid direct dissent.

> The avoidance of . . . open and bold negative expression is rooted in the fear that it might disrupt the harmony and order of the group, that it might hurt the feelings of a superior and that, in extreme circumstances, it could involve the risk of being cast out from the group as an undesirable member. Even if there are others who share a negative opinion, it is unlikely that they will join together and openly express it, for the fear that this might jeopardize their position as desirable group members.[6]

If one adds to these considerations the fact that the present Japanese management is quite old, with the top positions in

* A number of Indonesian planners told me how difficult it has proven for major Japanese oil companies quickly to formulate competitively effective bids in close international bidding. I strongly suspect that the lack of prompt Japanese response to the financial measures adopted by the Nixon Administration in August of 1971, as a result of which the Japanese had to absorb high financial losses, reflected the inability of the Japanese leadership to reach prompt decisions.

large businesses or corporations usually filled by men over sixty, one becomes less impressed by the Japanese decision-making process. In fact, I am rather inclined to think that the Japanese economy has worked well *in spite of,* and not because of, its internal decision-making mechanisms, and that in the setting of more difficult alternatives, greater pressures, or stronger competition, it will prove itself to be a severe handicap.

CAUSES REASSESSED

With these general considerations in mind, it may now be appropriate to take another look at the causes of the Japanese economic success to see which of them are likely to be applicable in the future, and to see also whether perhaps some additional new advantages may not materialize. It may be useful at this point to divide the twenty items into two broad categories, one essentially domestic in nature (subdivided, in turn, into those involving Japanese social conditions and values [A] and into those which are derived from deliberate decisions, practices, or policies [B]), and one basically involving foreign or international considerations.

Bearing our earlier observations in mind, it would appear that of the eight advantages listed in the first column, only number 6 (consumer demand) is likely to be fully operative

Table I. Causes of Economic Success

Internal		*External*
A	B	
1. Available labor	9. Governmental role	14. Low yen value
2. Work motivation	10. Corporate cooperation	15. Low defense costs
3. Low wages	11. Capital investment	16. U.S. paternalism
4. High savings	12. Role of banks	17. Free trade environment
5. Social stability	13. Exchange controls	18. Foreign technology
6. Consumer demand		19. Raw materials
7. Industrial sites		20. Korean and Vietnamese wars
8. Young elite		

in the decade of the seventies. Numbers 1 (labor) and 3 (wages) will be definitely negative; number 4 (high savings) may be adversely affected by inflation and by higher consumption of goods and is hence doubtful; all of the others appear doubtful for reasons already mentioned.

Of the five in the second column, three (9, governmental role; 12, the role of banks; and 13, exchange controls) are likely to be maintained, although the constructive role of government could be undermined by the political instabilities already noted, and exchange controls might be affected by foreign pressures. The remaining two (10, corporate cooperation; and 11, capital investment) are somewhat doubtful: the need to deal with domestic problems, given the relatively narrow range of profits in many Japanese corporations, may strain the corporate fabric and also reduce the capital available for investment; to be added to this is also the initially higher cost, before it begins to pay off, of a major domestic R & D effort.

Of the seven items of external origin, four (16, U.S. paternalism; 17, free trade environment; 18, foreign technology; and 20, the role of the Korean and Vietnamese wars) are likely to be inapplicable, while the remaining three are doubtful.

Thus, in an overall sense, the following picture emerges: of the twenty causes that cumulatively contributed to the Japanese economic success, during the decade of the seventies only four have a high probability of remaining operative; ten are doubtful, which is to say that there is at least a 50-percent chance that they will turn out to be negative; and six can be assumed to be negative.

An alternative way to make the evaluation would be to compress some of these items into fewer but broader categories:

1. Labor conditions (items 1, 2, 3).
2. Social behavior (4, 5, 6, 7).
3. Business behavior (8, 10, 11).
4. Government behavior (9, 12, 13).

Table II. Prospects for Economic Causes

	Internal A	*Internal* B	*External*
Positive:	6. Consumer demand	9. Governmental role 12. Role of banks 13. Exchange controls	
Doubtful:	4. High savings 2. Work motivation 5. Social stability 7. Industrial sites 8. Young elite	10. Corporate cooperation 11. Capital investment	14. Low yen value 15. Low defense costs 19. Raw materials
Negative:	1. Available labor 3. Low wages		16. U.S. paternalism 17. Free trade environment 18. Foreign technology 20. Korean and Vietnamese wars

5. U.S. role (14, 15, 16, 17, 20).
6. External opportunities (18, 19).

Of the above, it would appear that the third and the fourth are likely to be positive in the decade of the seventies, the second and the sixth are doubtful, and the first and fifth are negative.

Obviously, the above is somewhat mechanical, in that it treats the causes as more or less co-equal. That could hardly have been the case, but it is extremely difficult to determine which causes are more important than others, especially if it is judged that Japanese economic development has rested on an intricate interaction of domestic givens, subjective qualities, and deliberate Japanese actions, and of advantageous external circumstances. Nonetheless, guided in part by comments elicited from my Japanese interviews as well as by more expert judgments, it may be possible to hazard the following breakdown, selecting rather arbitrarily the following as the more immediate or critical causes of the Japanese economic success (using the same format as above):

Table III. "More Important" Causes of Economic Success

Internal A	*Internal* B	*External*
Available labor	Governmental role	Low defense costs
Work motivation	Corporate cooperation	Low yen value
Low wages	Capital investment	U.S. paternalism
Social stability		Free trade environment
		Foreign technology

We thus end up with seven internal and five external items. The breakdown, then, is as follows:

Of the seven internal, two are likely to be negative, four are doubtful, and one is positive. Of the five external, two are doubtful and three are negative. Cumulatively, of the twelve items selected as more crucial, one is likely to remain positive, six are doubtful, and five are negative.

Table IV. Cumulative Prospects for Economic Causes

	20 Causes of Japanese Success			12 "More Important" Causes		
	A *Internal*	B	*External*	A *Internal*	B	*External*
	8	5	7	4	3	5
Positive	1	3			1	
Doubtful	5	2	3	2	2	2
Negative	2		4	2		3

Of relevance here is the question of the relative importance of circumstantial, and particularly of external, factors to the Japanese success. This is not to gainsay the remarkable and admirable qualities of the Japanese: their capacity for hard work and their extraordinary intelligence. But it does appear on closer examination that these qualities made it possible for the Japanese to take advantage of favorable circumstances, without which the

Japanese performance might have been of an altogether lower magnitude. It is thus an error to ascribe to the Japanese the qualities of supermen and to ignore the rather uniquely advantageous circumstances they intelligently and industriously exploited. It is pertinent to recall here that the very same Japanese, with a similar pattern of decision-making, certainly with the same native industry and intelligence, on the eve of World War II, after several decades of most intensive efforts, were not ranked even among the top dozen nations in industrial production or capital.

PROSPECTS

Bearing all of these considerations in mind, it does seem proper to conclude that Japanese growth rates will slow down in the near future and that they will do so considerably below the levels of some of the more spectacular public prognostications, as well as below the more conservative official Japanese expectations. To be sure, there will be offsetting considerations at work also: relatively high growth rates will continue because of accumulated equipment and planned investment (second only to that of the United States); because of sheer momentum; because of the deliberate Japanese effort to spur domestic innovation; and also because the labor shortage will be somewhat offset by increased productivity and greater reliance on technology-intensive production. For example, Japan is making a most deliberate effort to develop in the computer field, and by the mid-seventies is likely to be a major computer producer, exporter, and user, challenging the American supremacy and placing herself ahead of all other states, except the United States.[7]

In addition, the domestic capital squeeze may be offset by a grudging liberalization, permitting the inflow of foreign capital, and some of Japan's industrial rivals may continue to falter. If America increasingly emphasizes frontier industries as well as software and know-how as its vital exports, in addition to agricultural products, the Japanese will be able to fill the vacuum, while their competitiveness may by itself strengthen America's inclination to opt out of the middle industrial range.

Nonetheless, on balance, I am quite skeptical—given the social and political, as well as foreign, factors already mentioned, in addition to more purely economic considerations—of Japan's ability to continue increasing her GNP at the extraordinary high rates of the last few years. This is not only a matter of dismissing the extreme projections, pointing toward Japan's economic global leadership; it is also to question the more modest but still very high official expectations of a growth of 10 percent per annum during this decade. It should be added that I consider it futile to speculate beyond that time range. Given the complexity and the interrelationship of the very variable and volatile factors that go into Japan's economic well-being, it is simply an exercise in speculation to project economic growth rates for more than a decade, not to speak of three, four, or five decades ahead.

In the light of the foregoing, my own general estimate—and it cannot be more than an estimate—is for an average growth rate of somewhere around (and perhaps even somewhat below) 8 percent per annum between 1970 and 1975, with perhaps a more marked slowdown developing around 1975 and thereafter, to an average of about 6 percent per annum between 1975 and 1980. This would give Japan a GNP of approximately $290 billion in 1975 and approximately $385 billion in 1980.*

* On an annual basis, with 1970 at $196 billion, the following approximate GNP (in billions of dollars) is indicated, assuming 8 percent per annum growth between 1970 and 1975, and 6 percent per annum growth between 1976 and 1980 (although these may be higher or lower in individual years).

1971	211	1976	305
1972	228	1977	323
1973	245	1978	343
1974	266	1979	364
1975	288	1980	385

It is uncertain that this growth—though still *very* impressive—will be enough to insure a sufficient margin for the resolution of Japan's domestic problems and for the maintenance of a very favorable trading position and industrial expansion. Indeed, it is more than likely that a certain squeeze will be felt, with resulting tensions in the definition of priorities, in allocation choices, or, more generally, in public policies. The likely economic picture, therefore, both approximates as well as intensifies the social and political prospects discussed earlier.

In an overall sense, the Japanese economy can be seen as now being in a phase of adjustment, from a period of rapid recovery to one of greater maturity, with that phase beginning to overlap with a phase of increasing complexity, not only for economic-technologic and scientific reasons, but also because of social and political pressures. These pressures, in their turn, will be much affected by Japan's overall international position, particularly by the degree of security or insecurity that that condition generates.

Part Two

International Problems

4

In Search of a Role

TWO BROAD OBSERVATIONS may usefully serve as the point of departure for our discussion of Japan's international position:

1. Though Japan is clearly ripe for something bigger than itself, the Japanese are encountering great difficulty in defining what that bigger role might be.
2. The growing sense of, and satisfaction from, national greatness clashes with the persisting—perhaps in some respects even heightened—sense of national insecurity, which complicates Japanese vision and causes further uncertainty in goals.

That the Japanese feel themselves ready to assume larger responsibilities is clear. That readiness, and even desire, emerges as a strong motif in private talks, is voiced quite openly in public discussions, and is articulated in official pronouncements. Most of the dialogue, for the time being, takes place within a framework that is largely of foreign origin and that, in its essence, involves living up to the image of Japan as the "good boy" of international politics. Hence there is much emphasis on Japan doing more to support the United Nations, or Japan assuming a larger role in international relief and other humanitarian activities, or Japan devoting an increasing share of her GNP to foreign aid.

yes

But beyond such pious declarations there are more serious, and earthly, discussions, based on the recognition that economic power is also, whether one wishes it or not, political power; and that Japan cannot therefore escape political responsibilities and hence the obligation to define its political goals. A good formulation of this point of view was stated in 1969 by the present Japanese ambassador to Washington (then serving as vice minister for foreign affairs):

> Even where "power" is primarily economic, once this reaches a certain magnitude, a nation's actions will come to possess political overtones and will produce political effects, even though this may be contrary to its intention. The Japanese people cannot ignore this principle which governs international society and merely seek their own economic development without assuming any political responsibility.[1]

The lead in these discussions has been taken by a group of foreign affairs experts, most of them professors or journalists. During the last several years, these men, most of whom have participated in many international conferences and have developed extensive contacts with Americans,* have contributed a great deal to stimulating Japanese awareness of Japan's potential role. In effect, they have launched, particularly through the medium of articles,† a public debate on the future directions of Japan's

* While their list is growing, the following come particularly to mind: Professor Masamichi Inoki, principal, Japanese Defense Academy; Professor Fuji Kamiya, Keio University; Professor Masataka Kosaka, Kyoto University; Professor Makoto Momoi, Defense Study Institute; Professor Kinhide Mushakoji, director of Sophia University's Institute of International Relations; Professor Michio Royama, Sophia University; Kiichi Saeki, director of Nomura Securities Research Institute; and Professor Kei Wakaizumi, Kyoto Sangyo University.

† During my stay in Japan I tried to compile a list of books that particularly influenced Japanese thinking on international affairs. To that end, I organized a somewhat select poll among a number of Japanese

foreign policy, awakening the Japanese public to the fact that its economic recovery inevitably carries with it much more complex political choices. Often viewed with some skepticism by the older Japanese statesmen, accustomed to operating in a setting of great reliance on the United States, these men have had a noticeable impact on the thinking of the younger Japanese political leaders, men like Tanaka or Nakasone and others.

This change in thinking, so far subtle but becoming more marked with time, is reinforced by the more pervasive reawakening of Japanese nationalism. As one keen Japanese observer has noted, "Japan's rapid economic growth has drastically magnified her self-confidence and intensified her nationalistic egocentrism, especially among the younger generation."[2] Mass consumption films and literature, both paying greater and more reverential attention toward things of the past, are but one example of a generally rising national consciousness and pride.* Such consciousness and pride—though at this stage lacking overt manifestations of national hatred for others—does provide a more direct political underpinning for an essentially insular and distinctively egocentric foreign orientation. The rising Japanese interest in assuming a larger role is thus motivated primarily by ego and self-interest; the predominant point of view, in spite of lip service to international "do-goodism," is that what is good for Japan is good . . . for Japan.

In other words, the rising concern with world affairs does not appear to be derived from a widespread recognition that a new global political process is taking shape, in which decisions will

---

writers on international affairs, both academic and journalistic. I quickly discovered that, to the extent that any books have been of importance, they have been of foreign origin; within Japan, most of the debate on international affairs and the more significant writings on international affairs have taken the form of lengthy articles.

* Perhaps a trivial but revealing example is that until recently the Japanese would give Western brand names to their various products, their television sets, washing machines, etc. Lately, much more typically and traditionally Japanese names have become increasingly popular.

increasingly have to be made in terms broader than the national interest. Rather, it rests on the argument that, since an economically powerful Japan confronts a new international situation, it must determine on its own how to relate itself to world affairs. In some cases, this might mean more independent activism, as in regard to China; in other cases, deliberate caution and a low profile are desirable. A good example of the latter is the Middle East, where the Japanese have a vital stake. Japan has been extremely reluctant to become involved, either in favor of the Arab or the Israeli side or in favor of more active support of a compromise settlement. Rather, as some Japanese have frankly intimated, the Japanese calculate that eventually the West will be driven from the region and a neutralist position will make it possible for Japanese interests to pick up the pieces.

AMBIGUITY AND INSECURITY

Thus, on the whole, though Japan is politically awakening, it is striking how consistently vague, uncertain, and ambivalent on specifics are the Japanese discussions of Japanese foreign goals. The presently ruling older generation has, in a way, one major advantage: it is very clear where it stands. It stands with the United States, behind the United States. Whether it does so out of habit or of self-interest or of calculated necessity is not important; what is important is that it is at least clear where it stands. The result is a halfway political position: though not explicitly defined as an indigenous Japanese policy, it is nonetheless a political position derived from an acceptance of a somewhat asymmetrical relationship with another power as the crucial point of departure for Japan's foreign policy.

That point of view, however, is becoming less dominant; it is becoming increasingly unacceptable psychologically and is being questioned also on pragmatic grounds. For a proud country, with an almost unprecedented history of continued existence as a nation, it is simply degrading to be, and to be seen (given the Japanese way of thinking, "to be seen" is even more important than "to be") as, a dependent of another major power. Moreover, Japanese economic recovery and America's simultaneous redefinition of its global responsibilities—or so many Japanese argue—dictate the necessity of Japan defining for itself a specific and more autonomous role in world affairs. Thus even the business community has urged publicly that the government

> produce outlines for a world policy formulation, but at the same time we should take steps to establish an effective and authoritative non-governmental organization dedicated to the formulation for the 70's of a world policy based on a new system of values. In this connection, the Council on Foreign Relations in the United States offers a good model.[3]

The Japanese tradition of judging social and political relations in hierarchical terms reinforces this trend toward greater self-assertion. It is striking for a foreigner to see a Japanese public opinion poll asking the Japanese public to rate their country on a scale ranging from a "first-rate nation" to a "tenth-ranked nation."* The very wording of the question confirms the shrewd observation made by Edwin Reischauer:

> They are usually either engaged in an attempt to catch up with some other country or else are vigorously trying to demonstrate their superiority to an unconvinced world. They feel that the eyes of the

* The poll, published in *Mainichi Shimbun* on August 15, 1970, asked the following question: "Before the war, Japan was said to be a first-rate nation. Immediately after the end of the war, it was said that Japan dropped to the level of a fourth-rate nation. What rate-nation do you think Japan is now, at the present time?" I should note here that the terms "first-rate" or "second-rate" really mean "ranked." The answers to the particular poll mentioned above indicate a somewhat greater inclination among older people to give Japan a higher ranking, but without marked generational deviations from the overall breakdown, in which 31 percent list Japan as a second-ranked nation, 32 percent as third-ranked, and 18 percent as first-ranked (with a perverse 1 percent of the younger people in the twenty-to-thirty age bracket listing Japan as a tenth-ranked or tenth-rated nation).

world are always upon them, not only when they venture abroad but also in their life at home. To the average Japanese, the actual indifference of the rest of the world to Japan would seem incredible. He assumes that the whole world is aware of and marvels at Japan's high rate of school attendance or whatever else he takes pride in, and that all foreigners are equally conscious and scornful of Japan's various shortcomings.[4]

In any case, it is probably fair to say that the majority of concerned Japanese (that is to say, those Japanese who are in one way or another concerned with foreign affairs, as well as those who are emotionally involved from a nationalist point of view) are searching for some new formula, for some new goals; in effect, they are finding that the other shore is not easy to reach. Defining Japan's goals and role is proving very difficult, and, as a result, the principal characteristic of the current Japanese discussions is their ambiguity.

To say this is not to ignore the various programs articulated by many different advocates. These range from essentially vague calls for a more global perspective to a catchall list of the various good and proper things that Japan should be doing; from a more concrete expression of the desire for greater independence from the United States to more specific moves toward China; from thinly veiled aspirations for the assumption of Asian leadership to either advocacy of unarmed or armed neutralism, including in some extreme cases the nuclear option. But what is missing is a more comprehensive effort to spell out how the world as a whole is changing, how Japan fits into that world, and what ought to be the balance between its interests and its responsibilities. As one thoughtful Japanese analyst of international affairs noted some years ago, "Japan is a special case, perhaps even unique, in that she has no 'natural' role to play."[5] Unlike West Germany, which could fulfill itself in a larger European community, Japan does not have a clear-cut, geographically determined setting for a creative role.

But there may be an even deeper, more complex, elusive, and intractable cause as well. Japanese society is run by a homogeneous establishment, deeply rooted in a traditional culture and philosophy and operating with an extraordinarily complex and structurally distinctive language; both factors very much influence the inner workings of the Japanese business, even while the latest techniques of modern science and technology are exploited to the fullest—in a word, a blend of universality of technique with a uniqueness of tongue and culture.[6] As a result, the Japanese find it extremely difficult to relate themselves meaningfully to the outside world and to define that relationship—to the extent that it is achieved—in terms other than self-centered. To be sure, all nations are self-centered in one way or another, but the difficulty that the Japanese encounter in overcoming this inclination appears to be greater and more complex. It stands in the way even when the Japanese deliberately wish to identify themselves with actions and activities of broader dimensions.*

This difficulty is maximized—and this is the second general observation—by the persisting and underlying sense of national insecurity. One would have thought that the extent of Japanese

* Symptomatic of this is the difficulty of finding good Japanese to serve in international organizations. Insular tradition and linguistic difficulties aside, the occupational structure of Japan is also such that "it is very hard to find a man to take a post in an international organization such as UNESCO or ECAFE. Although one can find able men who are interested in such positions, they would not be prepared to take the risk, in that they know that, once a short-term contract is completed, they would not be assured of finding a job back in Japan that is as good as or better than the position they would leave. . . . Japan's domestic system thus inhibits movement to international organizations; it also deters the really competent from participation in a new independent project, even if the term is limited" (Chio Nakane, *Japanese Society* [London: Weidenfeld and Nicolson, 1970], p. 107). In reverse, somewhat the same difficulty applies to foreign students, especially to those from the less developed countries, studying in Japan: linguistic barriers, cultural barriers, and the general homogeneity of the system do not permit the degree of integration that is achieved, despite other difficulties, in countries such as the United States or even those of western Europe.

dependence on good international relations would have generated a highly international elite, but in Japan it seems to have had the opposite effect of stimulating instead an outlook dominated by an inward-oriented anxiety, which reinforces the exclusivistic tendencies already noted. Japan is thus a highly internationally dependent country, led by an insular-oriented elite.

There are many good and rational reasons for the Japanese anxiety. Japan's geographic situation is politically not to be envied, immediate neighbors being the world's three giants and the world's principal nuclear powers. Surrounded by China's 800 million, the Soviet Union's 230 million, and America's 210 million, Japan in effect faces 1.2 billion people, or about 40 percent of the world's population, organized into three powerful states, two of whom are also the world's leading military and economic powers. This alone creates a situation of extraordinary vulnerability, which is made even worse both by Japan's relatively small size and by its susceptibility to natural disasters.

Added to this is the racial element. In spite of their impressive history, high culture, and national attainments—which make Japan truly one of the world's great nations—the Japanese convey a sense of racial sensitivity to the point of sometimes even rating themselves negatively in overall national physical appearance as compared to other peoples. This sense of racial identity, which merges with the national, prompts both assertiveness and apprehension in relationship to the outside world. There is a tendency to interpret outside criticism, especially American, as being racially motivated; in 1971 fears of an American reaction to Japanese export successes in the United States were frequently linked with apprehensive speculation about American anti-Japanese racial impulses.

Symptomatic of this insecurity, and more broadly of Japanese national narcissism, was the success in early 1971 of a rather strange best seller: a book by an unknown author, identified by the nom de plume Isaiah Ben Dasan, entitled *The Japanese and the Jews.* The book was widely discussed by the Japanese mass media, and most of the high officials (including the prime minister) with whom I talked had read the book. Its success was revealing of how the Japanese see themselves. The comparison with the Jews stressed the uniqueness of the two peoples, each endowed with special gifts and each therefore also subject to special global liabilities. The author warned the Japanese that the world is controlled by Christian and Communist *whites,* and, though in this world Japan is tolerated as an "honorary white," this toleration may not endure. Persecution may still be in store for the Japanese, as it has been for the Jews.

It would be an error to ignore these feelings of insecurity and of racial sensitivity. On the surface they are rarely evident, especially given the Japanese self-control, and, moreover, they are part of a larger web of impulses and drives that make the Japanese both so energetic and so able. Nonetheless, in more intimate relationships or in situations of greater stress, it is quite remarkable how quickly these particular feelings surface, providing a revealing glimpse into some of the more basic motivations driving the Japanese. Their existence, in turn, does suggest the enormous importance for foreigners to cultivate psychological subtlety when dealing with the Japanese, a factor that has sometimes been lacking in American-Japanese relations.*

The foregoing two broad considerations (persisting difficulty in defining clear-cut goals, despite Japan's "ripeness" for a bigger role, and the underlying sense of insecurity) make for a foreign policy that emerges very surreptitiously, largely by stealth, ex-

* It is widely believed in Japan that the U.S. secretary of commerce, Mr. Stans, is the unknown Nixon cabinet member cited by *Time* as having said: "The Japanese are still fighting the war, only now instead of a shooting war it is an economic war. Their immediate intention is to try to dominate the Pacific and then perhaps the world" (*Time,* May 10, 1971, p. 85). Remarks of this sort, especially if accompanied by a blustering style of negotiations, are good examples of what ought to be avoided.

perimentation, and cautious feel. As the Japanese begin to carefully inch away from under the American political umbrella (though not yet from under the strategic one), they are articulating a vague concept of a new Asian balance of power, in the context of which it may prove possible for Japan to continue to enjoy peace, to promote its economic well-being, and to enhance its international status.* This balance would involve the four major powers in the Pacific-Asian region: in addition to Japan, the United States, China, and the Soviet Union. In a general sense, it appears that the Japanese calculate that reasonably stable relations among these four major powers are possible, and that such a broad framework will prove compatible with the promotion of more specific Japanese economic and political interests (especially once the latter have been more precisely defined).

It may hence be accurate to characterize the present Japanese position with regard to foreign affairs as one of reexamination and recalculation. The basic postwar assumptions are being questioned, but new basic principles have not yet fully crystallized. Perhaps it would be more accurate to speak of a process of adjustment, an adjustment influenced above all by Japan's economic (and hence also psychological) recovery, and accelerated by the scaling down of America's global involvement, which many Japanese perceive the Nixon doctrine to symbolize. In the context of that process of adjustment, given the Japanese' own awareness of the ambiguity of their present formulations and

* A good example of the underlying thinking is contained in a thoughtful paper written some years ago by one of Japan's foremost students of international affairs, Professor Yonosuke Nagai: "We must make our choice on the basis of economic, political and geopolitical national interests, and in doing so we must assume that Japan is (1) fundamentally a status quo power, (2) situated in the Asian cultural bloc, (3) an advanced nation, and (4) a maritime state which, as long as the U.S. Seventh Fleet controls the Western Pacific, is destined to remain under America's nuclear umbrella" ("Japanese Foreign Policy Objectives in a Nuclear Milieu," *Journal of Social and Political Ideas in Japan* [April 1967], p. 29).

thinking, Japanese strategy at this stage can perhaps be best summarized as seeking *to maximize Japanese options and to diversify Japanese dependencies.*

AN ASIAN ROLE?

The strategy of maximizing options and diversifying dependencies has both economic and political aspects. In politics it means, in a nutshell, the cultivation of political relations other than primarily with the United States. In the economic realm it means a massive and even growing effort to widen still further and to make more secure Japan's access to foreign markets and raw materials. Despite the enormous successes so far attained (although more in the realm of trade than of foreign investments, in which the Japanese have lagged),* the Japanese are acutely aware of the high political vulnerability of many of their key sources of supplies. Only about one-third of Japanese foreign investments is in areas that can be considered as reasonably stable, and the overwhelming majority of that is in North America. Europe, contrary to the policy of diversification, accounts on the other hand for only about 5 percent.

Even more glaring, but also less subject to choice, is the situation prevailing with regard to raw materials. Most, inevitably, come from high-risk areas: for example, Japanese oil comes primarily from Iran, Saudi Arabia, and Kuwait (and at least two of these three are potentially very unstable) and iron ore mainly from Australia, India, Peru, and Chile (with three out of the four potentially unstable). To avoid excessive dependence,

* As of early 1971, Japanese foreign investments abroad amounted to about $2.7 billion. This was considerably less than the $71 billion for the United States, $17.8 billion for Great Britain, $4.7 billion for France, and $3.9 billion for Germany (the latter three as of 1968). (Mayasa Miyoshi, "Japan's International Trade and Investment Policies for the 1970s" [Paper read to a joint Keidanren–Atlantic Institute Conference, Tokyo, March 1971], p. 22.)

the Japanese have undertaken a concentrated effort to disperse their supplies, assigning—it seems—a higher priority to the areas with reasonably good prospects of social-political stability. This consideration, in addition to natural wealth, makes Australia extremely attractive, and the result has been a veritable explosion in Japanese-Australian economic relations, with some risk of an Australian backlash, since many Australians fear becoming Japan's Canada.*

The problem in defining the Japanese role in Asia is very relevant to these considerations, and it deserves more explicit commentary. For traditional reasons, including the already-mentioned racial factor, some Japanese are attracted by the notion of Japan assuming a special role in Asia. Whether that role is defined in benign terms (primary responsibility for helping other Asians to develop) or in more directly political terms (leadership of a political-economic grouping), the basic point is unambiguous. It means the creation of a zone of Japanese political and economic preeminence,[7] with a narrower inner zone in which Japanese security interests are closely intertwined with those of several Asian states (primarily South Korea, maybe Taiwan, and Indonesia, the latter in connection with the Straits

* Japan has already become Australia's biggest market. In 1969–70 Japan took 25 percent of Australian exports, the United States took 13.5 percent, and Britain took 11.9 percent. Japan took about half of Australia's mineral exports. Another area increasingly favored by the Japanese is Indonesia. India, on the other hand, seems to be losing its appeal. A leading Indonesian economic figure told me in late 1970 that a big change took place in Japanese attitudes sometime in 1969. The Japanese became much more willing to invest in projects designed to aid Indonesian development and not merely to promote Japanese economic interests. As a result, as of 1971 approximately one-third of all aid to Indonesia came from Japan and Japan became the biggest supplier of public-governmental aid to Indonesia. According to the Indonesians, Japanese businessmen are beginning to learn how to cooperate with Indonesians and to be less insistent on viewing all dealings with Indonesia from the standpoint of maximizing Japanese profits. The Japanese are becoming more willing now to invest in Indonesia in order to help them develop indigenous Indonesian industry.

of Malacca, through which flows most of Japan-destined oil).

The dependence of the Asian countries on Japan provides an obvious underpinning for some of this thinking. This dependence is clearly quite extensive, and it is growing. It has been estimated that the Japanese share of the Asian market will double between 1965 and 1975, from about 17 percent to about 35 percent, and there has already been some beneficial spinoff from Japan, encouraging the emergence of new, labor-intensive industries in Hong Kong, Taiwan, and South Korea, with Indonesia and perhaps South Vietnam, if it survives, shortly to follow suit.[8] Moreover, Japan has already become the principal supplier of foreign economic aid to several Asian countries, and its share in foreign aid is likely to increase, if present pledges are met.

Thus a special relationship is already in the making, with or without political—not to speak of security—initiatives, and it is being reinforced by a continuous growth of institutional links. But although the Japanese government is gradually overcoming the suspicions and even hostility with which many Asians have tended to approach Japan, it is nonetheless doubtful that this process will go so far as to permit the creation in the Asian context of a community in which Japan can define a meaningful political role for itself. Both subjective and objective deterrents stand in the way, and one might well wonder therefore whether Japan's best interests would actually be served by a deliberate Japanese effort to create such an Asian community.

On the subjective level, the impediments are both of Japanese and of non-Japanese origin. On the Japanese side, at least initially, the Japanese economic approaches to Asian countries were somewhat heavy-handed; they were openly characterized by the desire to extract maximum profit, taking the fullest advantage of Japan's favorable bargaining position. Japanese foreign aid, initially quite small and even in the Asian context itself less than that of the United States, has been marked by rather strict conditions, relatively more so than of most other donor countries.* Moreover, the Japanese on the whole are as contemptuous of most other Asians, especially of the Indians, as they occasionally tend to be deferential to the more powerful Westerners. As a result, on the non-Japanese side, complaints about Japanese selfishness and heavy-handedness, strong resentments of the "superior" attitude allegedly adopted by many Japanese businessmen, and the inclination of many Asians to view the Japanese as "honorary whites" have also reinforced the negative memories of World War II. In any case, in all my travels I have yet to meet an Asian who desires Japan to play a preeminent role in Asia.

In the longer run, the objective difficulties are likely to prove even more of an impediment. The basic and unchanging fact for the next several decades is that the real gap between Japan and the rest of Asia in the standard of living and in economic wealth will continue to widen.[9] This will also widen the cultural gap, diminishing the "Asianness" of Japan. Moreover, that gap is likely to be accompanied by persisting and perhaps even widening political disparities. Political instability in the various Asian countries will be of a different character and magnitude—both more violent and more chaotic—than the likely political changes in Japan, and this will further inhibit meaningful and more intimate collaboration.

I am therefore inclined to agree with those Japanese who have lately voiced skepticism concerning Japan's special role in Asia, in spite of Asia's cultural-racial attraction.[10] The Japanese might be better off avoiding such an undertaking; they should not be misled by nonexistent notions of an Asian identity or be

* The average redemption period (in years) of Development Assistance Committee (DAC) nations was 27.8; of these, the most generous period was offered by Canada, which averaged 48.5 years, and the lowest was that of Italy, which came to 10.6 years; the Japanese averaged 19.5 years, or lower than the DAC average. The DAC average interest rate was 2.8 percent; the highest was that of Italy, 4.2 percent, and Japan was second highest with 3.7 percent; Britain was most generous with 1.2 percent.

guided by essentially outdated concepts of geographical contiguity. The most the Japanese could accomplish in the Asian context, were they seriously to embark on the mission of forging a community in which they were to exercise political and economic leadership, would be to create for themselves what the United States, in part through historic inadvertence, obtained in Latin America: an area of predominance, but without solid political and social foundations—in a word, an economic empire built on political quicksand.

AWAY FROM GEOGRAPHY

Indeed, in some ways a better prospect for Japan, and in any case more in keeping with Japan's strategy of maximizing options and minimizing dependencies, involves economic relations with Latin America. This the Japanese are recognizing more and more, and a major Japanese economic effort is already underway. From the Japanese standpoint, Latin America offers a good or even a better target for their goods, for by and large Latin American needs are for somewhat more sophisticated products than are needed in the less developed Asian countries, and Latin America is at the same time an excellent source of raw materials. In Brazil, moreover, there is already a sizable Japanese presence, reinforced by the existence of a large Japanese immigrant community of some 600,000 to 700,000 people, and Japanese investments have been growing rapidly (from slightly over $200 million in 1969 to about $360 million in 1970, or a growth of 80 percent in one year).

In general, Latin America is becoming an area very attractive to Japanese direct investment, designed to insure for Japan enduring access to raw materials. Japanese trade with Latin America has also been expanding rapidly, a development that comes at a time when Latin America needs both sophisticated foreign know-how and capital, yet is more and more inclined to reduce or even reject the American presence. Unlike Asia, in Latin America local political needs and Japanese economic interests dovetail.* As a consequence, Latin America and Australia, rather than Asia, are becoming increasingly the El Dorados of Japanese businessmen.

Beyond that, the overall trend of Japan's economic involvement is not only away from a concentration on Asia,† but is pointing more and more toward an increasingly intimate involvement and interdependence with the advanced world. That Japan's economic relations with the United States are all-important (the Japanese trade with the United States amounts to about one-third of Japan's total trade) is a basic reality, and nothing in the foreseeable future, short of a calamitous break between the two states, is likely to alter this. In addition, however, the Japanese are becoming both more concerned and more aware of their need to develop closer economic relations with western Europe and particularly with the Common Market. This is the natural outcome of the increasing sophistication of Japanese industrial processes, and it has already involved a marked and apparently continuing shift in Japanese trade from low-income areas to higher-income areas.‡

* "Japan's phenomenal economic growth in the past decade, with its voracious demand for industrial raw materials, has already been responsible for a substantial shift of trade of all other Pacific countries from the Atlantic to the Pacific, and projections suggest that this trend will continue and intensify, based on projected growth rates of the Japanese economy at 10–12% per annum, for at least another decade. Japan's growth will dwarf all other possible developments and policies in bringing about closer trans-Pacific economic relations and diversification to Latin American trade and investment" (H. W. Arndt, "Economic Cooperation in the Pacific: A Summing Up" [paper read at Conferencia del Pacifico, Vina del Mar, Chile, September 27–October 3, 1970], p. 11).

† In 1938 38 percent of Japanese imports and 60 percent of Japanese exports were with South and Southeast Asia; in 1954 imports amounted to 19 percent and exports 28 percent; in 1963 imports had shrunk to 14 percent and exports had fallen to 18 percent.

‡ In the years 1934–36 the low-income areas absorbed 72.9 percent of Japanese exports; the high-income areas amounted to only 27.1 percent. In 1950 the respective percentages were 60.9 percent and 39 percent. In 1960 the percentages were 53.2 percent and 46.8 percent. In 1968

For Japanese financial circles, the Japanese–American–(West) European relationship already represents the crucial triangle. It is in the International Monetary Fund, in the Group of Ten, in the Organization for Economic Cooperation and Development (OECD) that crucial decisions, affecting Japan's overall economic welfare, are made, and it is with London, Zurich, Brussels, as well as Washington and New York, that Japanese bankers and financiers are in continuous and increasingly personal touch. The world financial community thus rests on three pivots, and its existence epitomizes Japan's intimate and central involvement in the advanced part of the world, geography notwithstanding.

This development heightens the importance to the Japanese of international economic and particularly fiscal arrangements. How to reconstruct the GATT has been a particularly perplexing problem because on the one hand the Japanese are anxious to obtain greater access to European markets, yet on the other hand their insular and inward orientation makes them unwilling to open their own doors fully to West European and American products. Largely out of fear of an American overreaction to imbalances in trade between the United States and Japan, the Japanese have belatedly begun to accelerate their liberalization, but the basic reality is still one of unwillingness to do so; only as much is done as appears to be necessary, largely because of political pressures. The Japanese relationship with the advanced world is hence incongruous: Japan's ties with it are growing, but the Japanese have lagged in developing a relevant two-way free trade mentality.

Moreover, the Japanese have so far been slow both in foreign investment and in their actual participation in the so-called

---

they were 46.9 percent and 53 percent. See Warren Hunsberger, "The Japanese Economy: A Continuing Miracle?" *Interplay*, December 1969–January 1970, p. 18. Japanese exports to western Europe grew in 1970 by 42 percent over 1969, and represented the highest increase in Japanese foreign trade. Exports to the United States grew by 20 percent; to Southeast Asia by 10 percent (*Japan Economic Journal*, July 13, 1971).

multinational corporations. To catch up, the Japanese are likely to embark on an accelerated program of foreign investment, both in the high-income areas and in a few chosen less developed countries. Some Japanese economic officials have estimated that "it is considered necessary for Japan to raise such investment an average of 50 percent annually over the next six years."[11] Increasing Japanese investment in Europe is particularly to be expected. Japanese firms and hotels are already evident in the major European centers, and the next decade will doubtless see a very rapid growth in the Japanese presence in West Europe. Such accelerated investment carries with it the attendant risk that the Japanese, having already done extremely well in competitive trade, will now be accused of attempting "to buy up the world." They may also try to step up their involvement in multinational enterprises but, because of their limited experience and cultural impediments, they are not likely to do so quite as rapidly as may be desirable from the standpoint of their own interests.

In any case, such increasing economic involvement with the advanced world, though highlighting the point that Japan's ambitions cannot be defined in a narrow Asian regional framework, does not constitute by itself an answer to the question of Japan's proper role. To the extent that it remains primarily an economic relationship, the growing involvement with the more advanced world and with Latin America leaves unanswered the question of a nationally satisfying political role. Before examining the possibility of buttressing that relationship with a more meaningful political framework, a word or two must be said about Japan's relations with its Communist neighbors.

RELATIONS WITH RUSSIA

With Asia a dubious object for an active Japanese policy, for some Japanese China and/or the Soviet Union may loom as attractive targets, if not for a special Japanese role then at least for a special relationship.

Of the two, relations with the Soviet Union involve fewer cultural, emotional, and political complications. The Japanese do not like the Russians. More than that, they have strong feelings of resentment and contempt for them, possibly disliking them as a nation more than they do any other. The resentment may strike a Westerner as surprising, but it is derived from the feeling (which the Japanese frequently express) that the Russians stabbed Japan in the back in 1945, when Japan was practically on its knees, despite a nonaggression treaty concluded only a few years earlier. The contempt is derived from the view that basically the Russians are crude and inefficient to boot. Moreover, the Japanese soundly defeated the Russians in a one-to-one contest, a victory of which the Japanese are still proud. As a consequence, all public opinion polls reveal a consistently low ranking for the Soviet Union.*

To the factors mentioned at the outset, there is to be added the element of widespread recollection that literally hundreds of thousands of Japanese prisoners of war in Soviet hands were never returned and presumably perished because of Soviet mis-

* For instance, to the question, "With which country do you think Japan must be most friendly from now on—please list one country," only 3 percent identified the Soviet Union; the highest ranking was obtained by the United States, with 42 percent, (*Asahi Shimbun,* January 14, 1970). To the question, "On which country do you think Japan should be modeled?," only 2 percent identified the Soviet Union; the highest rankings were obtained by the United States and Switzerland, each polling 29 percent (Mainichi Poll, cited by *The Economist,* August 29, 1970). To the question, "If you were able to go to any country you liked freely, which would you like to visit the most?" only 4 percent identified the Soviet Union. The highest ranking was obtained by Western Europe, with 46 percent (*Mainichi Shimbun,* April 30, 1971). Also, most public opinion polls indicate that, when asked to identify the main enemy of Japan, the largest number by far identifies the Soviet Union. When asked to pick the main friend, a very small minority picks the Soviet Union, with China doing considerably better, but with the United States by far the most frequent choice.

or Mylai ?

treatment or worse (shades of Katyn?), and to some Japanese the question of the Hokkaido offshore islands is still a live issue. However, on the latter point, my impression is that it is more of a live issue in Hokkaido itself, where even road signs and television blurbs periodically remind the Japanese of the illegal Soviet retention of the four offshore islands; elsewhere in Japan, the issue seems somewhat inconsequential though useful to the Japanese in their bargaining with the Soviets. However, with rising nationalism, and especially after the return of Okinawa, the issue may acquire more vitality. Currently, more lively than the Hokkaido offshore islands is the issue of the fisheries and fishermen. Soviet treatment of the Japanese fishermen fishing in the Kuril region has been extremely harsh, occasionally verging on the brutal.* Finally, there is a widespread suspicion of Soviet motives and a realization, especially on the elite level, that any excessive cultivation of relations with the Soviet Union could rebound against Japanese-American relations. The underlying attitude, therefore, is one of suspicion, which does not exclude the development of clearly calculated relationships, but relationships precisely measured to fit Japanese interests.

Practicality is thus the decisive principle governing the Japanese approach toward the Soviet Union. The Japanese recognize that the Soviet Union is a very major neighbor, a potentially devastating threat, the principal rival of Japan's closest foreign partner, and prospectively an excellent customer for Japanese industry as well as a conveniently located supplier of raw ma-

* Between the years 1946–1969, the Soviet Union seized 1,314 Japanese fishing vessels and 11,126 Japanese fishermen; of these, 810 ships and 10,682 fishermen were returned. Twenty-one ships were sunk, and 32 fishermen were killed. That these incidents do not date back merely to the early stages of the cold war is suggested by the following data: in 1968 40 ships and 345 fishermen were captured, and 15 ships and 298 fishermen were returned; in 1969 39 ships and 363 fishermen were captured, and 12 ships and 311 fishermen were returned, 2 ships were sunk and 12 fishermen were killed (R. Shiratori, in *Peace Research in Japan,* Tokyo, 1970, p. 46).

terials. Moreover, the Japanese know that the Soviet Union has several major interests in Japan, which incline the Soviet Union to cultivate better relations with Tokyo. There is, first of all, the need for Japanese technology and capital, particularly for Siberian development, a need that places the Soviet Union vis-à-vis Japan almost in the position of an underdeveloped country; secondly, the Soviet Union's fear of China enhances the importance to Moscow of good relations with Japan, not only as a balance but perhaps also in order to inhibit too exuberant a Japanese plunge into aid and trade with China; thirdly, the Soviet desire to reduce American-Japanese intimacy tempts Moscow to play subtly on Japanese nationalistic feelings, although very carefully, for Soviets know that they are dealing here with a Pandora's box.

A tantalizing question is how far the Soviets would wish to undermine the American-Japanese relationship. That it should be less intimate probably appears automatically desirable to any apparatchik in the Kremlin. But a Japan detached from the United States and clearly much too powerful and nationally ambitious to become the Soviet Union's Far Eastern Finland could quickly find itself attracted by the idea of massive rearmament. Hence, a more sophisticated Soviet political thinker may also be inclined toward caution and even see some desirability in continued American-Japanese intimacy. Soviet studies of Japan, published in the more thoughtful and less propagandistic organs, do reveal a sophisticated understanding of Japan's growing power—as well as more than just a touch of anxiety over its longer-run implications.

The interplay of these interests and motivations makes inherently for a more active Tokyo-Moscow relationship. Formal diplomatic relations have thus become more benign in recent years. In addition, the Japanese have also set up a number of "front organizations" whose task it is to cultivate and explore the opportunities involved in better Soviet-Japanese relations. This has been done with typical Japanese subtlety. A variety of institutes and committees have been established to promote trade, scientific, and cultural contacts with the Soviet Union. Typically headed by semiretired senior members of the Japanese business-government establishment, ostensibly these outfits are reminiscent of some Western left-of-center organizations, proselytizing better relations with the Communist states.

In the Japanese case, however, the approach is much more level-headed and hard-nosed. These outfits (with the exception of those sponsored directly by left-wing political parties) are really government front organizations, pursuing the Japanese interests coldly and with calculation, in close consultation with the government. This makes in practice for relatively slow movement, as many exasperated Soviets in Tokyo at times complain, but it does mean that, though the issue is pursued, it is pursued prudently, with deliberation.

A good example is the question of Soviet raw materials. The Japanese, for obvious reasons, find Siberia attractive. Its natural wealth and proximity make it an obvious target for Japanese economic exploitation. Yet, at the same time the Japanese have no inclination to become so dependent on Soviet supplies as to give the Soviets a political bargaining lever. According to the estimates of one of the key sponsors and participants in Japanese-Soviet trade talks, by 1980 Japanese reliance on Soviet trade supplies (on the big assumption that Japanese-Soviet trade relations will unfold smoothly) would amount at most to approximately 10 percent of the total imports of iron ore and coal, 12 percent of lumber, and 3 percent of crude oil, with the overall trade amounting to about 5 percent of Japan's total. Trade at that level, to be sure, will not be insignificant, but it will still not be a matter of dependency; moreover, the Soviet Union in return would acquire a corresponding and perhaps even potentially greater dependence on more sophisticated Japanese products.

Japanese anxiety over the potential Soviet military threat to Japan is a further limiting factor. That threat, on the one hand, induces the Japanese to seek as normal relations with Moscow as possible, and trade is certainly an important aspect of such a normal relationship. A high Soviet stake in good relations with Japan presumably would diminish the Soviet inclination to threaten Japan. On the other hand, the potentiality of that threat (for example, the Japanese have been following avidly, but noncommittally, the Western debate over the meaning of the expanding Soviet role in the Indian Ocean and studying closely the relationship of the Soviet military rivalry with the United States to the Soviet threat to Japan) makes many Japanese reluctant to promote economic ties with the Soviet Union on such a scale as to contribute materially to Soviet economic power and scientific sophistication.

Thus, although in principle agreements concerning the joint development of Siberia have been reached, one may expect a steady but not a spectacular growth in Japanese-Soviet trade. Two-way trade may reach somewhere around $5.1 billion during the period 1971–75, almost doubling the $2.9 billion attained in 1966–70, which means that the annual rate of growth in that trade will remain fairly steady, at approximately 12.5 percent over the entire ten-year period.

Expansion might have been more rapid if Japanese caution had not been matched by Soviet paranoia and greed. All the Japanese businessmen who have dealt with the Russians complain of excessive Soviet secrecy, making it difficult to conduct unhindered on-the-spot surveys and delaying access to needed data. Soviet bureaucratic inefficiency is a further stumbling block, as is the Soviet desire to extract from the Japanese extremely favorable credit terms, essentially on the same level as those granted by advanced countries to less developed nations. The Japanese are simply not inclined to grant such terms.[12]

The Soviet Union thus offers at best a somewhat tempting economic opportunity, but one tempered by emotional and political considerations. One should not expect spectacular Japanese moves, even though it is likely that Moscow will choose, as an answer to the new Washington-Peking flirtation, to step up some of its initiatives toward Japan. In this connection, it is noteworthy that Soviet analyses of Japanese developments are comprehensive and analytically sophisticated, in striking contrast to the rather primitive Soviet handling of Chinese affairs. The Japanese response, though formally positive and even superficially cordial, will remain limited by strong feelings of suspicion and caution. The Soviet Union accordingly is not where Japan will seek to fulfill herself.

THE LURE OF CHINA

China is a different story. Here, Japanese emotions are more mixed, Japanese aspirations more ambitious, the interplay of external policies and domestic Japanese politics more complex. Public opinion polls concerning China show a much more favorable popular attitude than toward the Soviet Union.* The dominant attitude toward China and the Chinese (leaving aside for

* Thus, roughly one-half fewer Japanese identify China as the likely enemy of Japan than the Soviet Union; half again as many are likely to identify China as the main friend of Japan in contrast to the Soviet Union, although both lag very considerably behind the United States. In response to the earlier cited question, "On which country do you think Japan should be modeled?" China does not do any better than the Soviet Union, and neither does she do much better than the Soviet Union in response to the question, "If you were able to go to whatever country you liked freely, which would you like to visit the most?" However, in response to the question, "With which country to you think Japan must be most friendly from now on?" China ranked second after the United States, polling 21 percent of the vote. A comprehensive public opinion poll on Japan's foreign policy conducted by *Yomiuri* in May 1970 (published May 31, 1970) indicated widespread sentiment in favor of better relations between Japan and China, although almost 19 percent felt that Chinese nuclear development is a serious threat to Japan, with an additional 40 percent indicating that they feel it to be "a threat to some extent."

the moment the ideological problem or the question of Taiwan) is that of sympathetic fascination, of cultural and racial kinship (with a slight dose of an inferiority complex), and a sense of war guilt. The Japanese appear to admire and respect the Chinese. There is also some fear, too, but that, for the moment and in part at least, is offset by Japan's far greater economic power.

Many Americans assume that Japan and China are, if not natural adversaries in the Asian context, then at least natural rivals. Whatever the truth of that assumption may actually be, the Japanese-Chinese relationship appears in a different light to many Japanese. With the underlying sense of racial kinship serving as a point of departure, many Japanese tend to think both of Japan and of China as victims of the more powerful Western white nations, ranging from Americans through the European invaders to the Russians. Moreover, many Japanese tend to assume that there is a certain fundamental complementarity between Japan and China: Japan, an advanced industrial power, is a maritime nation, thrusting outward into the Pacific; China, a retarded, essentially agricultural society, is a land mass, with its population pressures pointing either northward or southward. There is thus no fundamental clash between the two, and, in many respects, each can benefit by a closer association with the other.*

Unlike the Soviet Union, China is also a live domestic issue in Japanese politics. As a result, it is less easy for the Japanese government and business to handle relations with China with the

* It is interesting to note that the Russians, the closest neighbor of the two, also think so. Japan as a superstate was the theme of a book published back in 1900, written by the Russian historian-philosopher Vladimir Soloviev. Entitled *Three Conversations on War, Progress and the End of World History*, it describes an industrially and technologically advanced Japan, linked up with China, engaging in a conflict with Russia (whose oppressed non-Russian peoples rise up in revolt), and subsequently overrunning not only Russia but even Europe. Some of the current Soviet reactions to Japanese militarism, to Chinese militancy—and to American diplomacy—are in the same tradition.

same degree of cold calculation as relations with the Soviet Union. Domestic political pressures and emotions make the matter highly volatile, and the Chinese government has not been above the temptation to play skillfully on Japanese emotions.

Thus, although the Japanese have also established semiofficial "front organizations" to deal with the Chinese,* it has been difficult for the Japanese to calibrate carefully an improvement of relations with China against the growing Japanese economic stake in Taiwan,† and in keeping with the simultaneous thaw in U.S.-Chinese relations. Instead, there have been rising pressures for more rapid movement, advocated by different groups for different reasons: the intellectual community, out of a mixture of ideological-cultural-racial motivations; the business community, out of the desire to beat the United States and western Europe to the Chinese markets; the politicians, to prove themselves to the public as forward-looking and independent-minded; and some policy makers, as a way of enhancing Japan's international standing.

Some of the policy makers had toyed—prior to the July 1971 announcement of Nixon's forthcoming visit to Peking—with the idea of a "division of labor" between Japan and the United States: the United States for the time being would maintain its ties with Taiwan, while Japan would pave the way by moving ahead with the normalization of relations with Peking. The sudden leap forward in American-Chinese relations has shown Japan that neither Washington nor Peking need Tokyo as an "honest broker," but this is likely to precipitate even greater

* For example, Fujiyama's mission to China—the so-called China Memorandum Trade Committee—is actually staffed by "detached" officials from MITI and the Foreign Ministry, including one official stationed semipermanently in Peking, even though Fujiyama himself opposes Sato's leadership in the LDP. A key and extremely able former senior MITI official active in this group is Mr. Yaeji Watanabe. Genuinely concerned with improving Japanese-Chinese relations, he is regarded as the likely first Japanese ambassador to Peking.

† Japanese interests control about 60 percent of Taiwan's foreign trade, while direct Japanese-Taiwanese trade is roughly equal to that between mainland China and Japan.

Japanese anxiety to move forward, and perhaps even to leapfrog America, in their relations with China.

The desire for a basic reorientation of Japanese policy toward China is strongest in the journalistic-academic circles. Of course, the JSP has been advocating such a move for a long time. The Komeito and the SDP have favored it as well, though less vociferously. These parties, however, speak largely to, and on behalf of, fairly cohesive but still minority blocs of the electorate, and thus their views tend to be taken for granted. The public clamor of the journalistic community and of the academics, while not new in substance, is something much more visible, and, linked to the internal conflicts within the LDP and intensified by the U.S. initiative toward China, it is generating momentum.

Japan will thus soon have to confront some very difficult choices. The Taiwan issue is likely to become an especially painful one. Many Japanese leaders have close ties with Taiwan, either through economic links or personal connections with the Taipei leadership or because of national sympathy for Taiwan. Indeed, the Taiwanese nationalist movement has been tacitly supported by the Japanese. Many Japanese, one suspects, would like to see a Taiwanese Taiwan, which could quietly become a Japanese security protectorate and an extension of the Japanese economy. The discovery of oil in the Chinese Nationalist-claimed islands of Senkaku (off Okinawa) heightens the potential importance of a separate Taiwan, for a reunited China would be in a stronger position to press Chinese claims. Strong emotions and high interests are thus involved in the question of Taiwan, and they will continue to complicate the Japanese desire to establish closer links also with Peking.

Nonetheless, painful as it will be, pressures to break relations with Taiwan altogether are likely to become irresistible after Peking's admission to the United Nations. However, even then it is rather difficult to see what the real meaning of any special Tokyo-Peking relationship might be, once diplomatic relations have been established and once, somehow, the Taiwan issue has been put aside. With the exception of the leftists, who favor a Chinese-Japanese alignment based on ideology and that therefore could be attained only if Japan were to turn toward socialism at home, the advocates of a basic change are left essentially with atmospherics and economics.

Change in atmospherics would satisfy for a while the residual Japanese craving for some Asian fulfillment, as well as the desire to do something on the international scene without—even despite—the United States. But one is justified in wondering how long that would last and how satisfying that would be. Once the initial glow fades, what really would have been accomplished? Most Japanese do not desire to strain the U.S.-Japanese relationship as an end in itself, though occasionally they are now more prepared to strain it on behalf of their own interests. Hence, self-assertion vis-à-vis the United States would provide at most a passing and ephemeral satisfaction. Moreover, to the extent that the United States, at least for the moment, has moved ahead of Japan on the Chinese question, the Japanese task is not self-assertion vis-à-vis the United States, but rather catching up or being left isolated. Beyond that, it is hard to conceive lasting Japanese-Chinese political cooperation (on what, for whom, against whom, why?) without, as already noted, major domestic changes in one society or the other.

That leaves economics, and this is where the matter becomes much more concrete. For many Japanese businessmen, the Chinese market offers an irresistible lure. Its very scale is magnetic.*

* This sometimes even leads to absurd calculations. Thus the economic editor of a serious paper (whom, out of politeness, I will not identify) engaged in the following "market analysis": "Suppose one in a hundred people in China decides to own a car. The total will add up to 7.5 million. Japan's annual car production volume is about 5.3 million, including midget four-wheeled cars. Our largest overseas market—the United States—imports only 460,000 cars from Japan. The size of the Chinese market will be clear from this example." Not a word on how economic allocations are made in China; not a word on the fact that it would take more than ten years of the average Chinese's income to buy a Japanese car.

Moreover, there are businesses in Japan that stand to gain from a major expansion in Chinese-Japanese trade, especially those in steel, shipbuilding, automobiles, fertilizers, and chemicals. In return, the Chinese could increase their exports of agricultural items and products from their fisheries; indeed, in the event of a major effort to expand trade, Chinese exports of these items could affect adversely the current Japanese purchases of soybeans from the United States, and place in jeopardy the Japanese fishing industry.

However, a qualitative change in the scale of the present Japanese-Chinese trade (which, it should be recalled, exists and has been growing, in spite of the absence of formal diplomatic relations—hence it is not a matter of "to trade or not to trade") would require rather major Japanese credits, which, in turn, given the Japanese economic structure, would have to involve a major policy decision. Alternatively, the initiation of more normal Japanese-Chinese relations could be accompanied by Japanese reparations (which Chiang Kai-shek had waived on China's behalf) to the mainland. However, as one intimate participant in Japanese-Chinese negotiations observed, reparations may not be a desirable way to initiate better relations: they are not likely to be big enough to compensate the Chinese for the blood spilled and the sufferings inflicted, yet they are likely to be too big not to generate some Japanese resentments.

Credits is the only way, and soft credits, on very favorable terms, would certainly be required by the Chinese. This means, in effect, that one portion of the Japanese economy will be subsidizing the expansion into China of another portion of the Japanese economy. Under normal circumstances that might be quite acceptable, even competitively desirable, and the popular mood concerning Japanese-Chinese relations almost certainly would favor some special arrangements. On the other hand, it is very likely that for some time to come the governmental officials in charge of economic affairs will resist the granting of special favors to China on the ground that there are no special economic reasons for so doing. Even a relatively minor economic squeeze and slowdown in Japan's economic growth would further reduce the Japanese inclination to be generous.

On their side, the Chinese so far have not been very tractable. Outwardly they have projected an air of amiability and accommodation, but in actual negotiations with the Japanese they have been quite tough. Japanese negotiators, including the China Memorandum Trade Committee members, have been obliged to sign self-denigrating declarations.* Chinese attacks on Japanese "militarism" have lately become more, rather than less, intense, and Japanese firms that wish to deal with Peking must denounce their economic ties with Taiwan (although some of the Japanese firms evade these restrictions by creating "independent" subsidiaries to deal with Taiwan). Japanese businessmen who have had extensive dealings with the Chinese and who themselves favor rapid movement by Tokyo toward Peking privately concede that the development of trade with China is likely to prove even more difficult than with the Soviet Union.

Accordingly, it is difficult to make precise estimates of the likely volume of Japanese-Chinese trade, though it will doubtless grow. In addition to the obstacles noted, there is the fundamental matter of widening economic disparity. As Japan moves into an increasingly sophisticated stage in its scientific-technological development, its trade will tend to emphasize more and more items needed by other advanced economies. To be sure, this is not true of all sectors of industry, and for some, China will be an excellent outlet. But a massive, explosive expansion in Japanese-Chinese trade is not likely, even under the best political-commercial circumstances. The Japanese political-business

* The 1958 Principle of Non-Separation of Politics from Trade, the 1959 Three Political Principles, the 1963 Trade Principles, the 1970 Four Conditions have all provided a Chinese-dictated political-ideological framework for economic arrangements between China and Japan.

circles directly concerned with the promotion of Japanese-Chinese relations estimate privately that, assuming favorable developments, Japanese-Chinese trade will double or triple between 1970 and 1975 (i.e., it will range from about $1.6 billion to $2.5 billion per annum); some hope that by 1980 it might be much higher than that, reaching by then the level of one-third of U.S.-Japanese trade (which would mean roughly 10 percent of Japan's total trade).

One is therefore justified in concluding that China will continue to attract many Japanese; that efforts to make the political relationship more intimate will persist, but without reaching the level of close political cooperation; that trade will grow and assume a more important role, though its growth will actually make such trade more important to Peking than to Tokyo (a fact that the Japanese do not seem to take into sufficient account in their dealings with the Chinese), but without fulfilling the more dramatic expectations sometimes voiced by Japanese enthusiasts of a special Tokyo-Peking relationship. Short of a crisis in relations with America (of which more later), which pushes Japan into Chinese arms on the rebound, the probable emergence of a more normal relationship between Tokyo and Peking will mean something less than intimacy, though something more than isolation. In a word, China is likely to prove a bigger temptation than an opportunity.

Our discussion of Japanese relations with the Soviet Union and China has not dealt with the question of security. That issue is clearly a sensitive one, and one that preoccupies a great many Japanese. It warrants separate consideration, which will now follow. However, it is relevant to note at this juncture that to the extent that the Japanese feel themselves physically threatened, the threat originates primarily from the Soviet Union and China. Growth in Chinese nuclear power is beginning to give the Japanese second thoughts, even though initially there was some tendency to dismiss it—and even, among a few, to take a little bit of pride in an Asian power forcing its way into the exclusively white nuclear club. The sense of danger is an additional argument for more normal relations with both Communist states, but it does, in the final analysis, work against any far-reaching intimacy. Thus neither Communist state—though of the two China is much the more alluring—offers Japan the opportunity for a special political role.

5

Security and Status

THE JAPANESE APPROACH to the question of national defense seems to be motivated by a mixture of genuine security concerns with a more elusive preoccupation with international standing. This combination makes it more difficult to answer the questions: How far will Japan rearm and, above all, will she go nuclear?

Basically, Japanese security policy will be shaped, first of all, by the Japanese reading of the Washington-Peking-Moscow triangle. On this rational level, the Japanese will monitor closely the changes in that relationship, particularly as they affect Japan's security. This means making subtle political judgments concerning intentions, reliability, and goals of the major powers, as well as more specific estimates of relative balances of power, military capabilities, disposition of forces, and the like. Secondly, on the less rational or, if you will, more subconscious level, Japanese security policy will also be shaped by Japanese national ambitions; thus it will be influenced by the Japanese estimate of their relative international standing, either with or without great military power, by the national desire to rank higher in the global pecking order, by the pride that some Japanese take in their military traditions, and by the emotional link between patriotism and the uniform. Thirdly, domestic social-political as well as economic developments will also influence Japanese security policy. The interplay of these factors will affect popular attitudes, either enhancing or moderating the desirability of a major military program.

Though it is difficult to judge, it is probably true that the Japanese sense of insecurity (speaking now strictly in the defense sense) has not significantly declined, despite the apparent waning of the cold war or the thaw in U.S.-Chinese relations. Working against this decline are two fundamental developments: (1) less certainty of American protection, especially given the relative decline in American power vis-à-vis Japan's potential opponents and the acquisition by the Japanese of a sense of national wealth, which is dependent almost entirely on external protection and which makes Japan a worthy target of envy, blackmail, or threat; and (2) the more general uncertainty concerning world trends, of which the Japanese are becoming more sensitive as they more massively enter the world.

OPENING THE DOORS

Japanese defense efforts so far have been modest. A small defense force is in existence, capable of limited coastal and of nearby air and sea operations. It is certainly not capable of undertaking any major operations on its own, and its capacity for home defense, assuming the somewhat unlikely probability of a conventional invasion, would not go beyond four or so weeks. To be sure, the quality of the existing formations is in many respects quite high. I was very favorably impressed by the morale, energy, and discipline of the units I had the opportunity of inspecting.* Their maintenance and overall technical competence seemed to be of a very high order, and their ability to handle complex command-control systems and most modern weaponry certainly is not to be doubted (given corresponding Japanese economic achievements). It is also the case that, on a unit-by-unit comparison, the Japanese have a higher ratio of combat men to logistical support forces than the United States, and it is probable that the Japanese military, all volunteers, would fight more intensely than their U.S. counterparts.

Yet, in an overall sense, the existing Japanese units, especially the land units, can hardly be considered a modern striking force. Their training seems to be designed primarily for World War II type operations, with heavy emphasis on coastal defense against a World War II type landing operation. There is much emphasis on tanks, and apparently so far, at least, little on helicopters (although that is about to change). It is uncertain how much actual training land forces have had for nuclear attack or for sustained guerrilla or counter-guerrilla warfare. Their equipment and tactics convey, in general, a rather anachronistic impression.

Moreover, the development of the Japanese SDF does not appear to be overtly guided—as far as one can see—by any comprehensive strategic concept, relating in a coherent fashion Japan's political situation, geopolitical setting, its own means and those of its potential adversaries and allies, to Japanese defense needs. Japanese land forces seem to be geared to fighting off a Soviet invasion conducted on the American patterns of a quarter-century ago. The senior field commanders talk largely in terms reminiscent of World War II; defense thinkers in Tokyo, on the other hand, seem very much up to date on the latest

* Thanks to arrangements made by the head of the Japanese Self-Defense Forces Agency, I was able to spend some time with the Northern Army, the elite formation of the Japanese ground SDF, charged with the defense of the strategically vital island of Hokkaido.

American strategic developments and weaponry, but between the two there seems to be a striking gap.

The SDF, organized as it is into separate air, sea, and land services, and with its table of organization largely patterned on the United States, seems to be more a replica of what once used to be considered the normal defense structure (and of what is still needed by a major land-sea continental power like the United States) than of what is now needed by a territorially confined and vulnerable chain of islands. One would have thought that a functionally organized and organizationally integrated single defense service would have been the logical way for the Japanese to approach their defense problem.*

It is to be expected, however, that the next several years will see qualitative improvement in the Japanese SDF. Particularly under the energetic leadership of Yasuhiro Nakasone (the head of the SDF until the summer of 1971), major strides were taken in the direction of modernizing the Japanese defense forces and developing a relevant defense concept. Although direct military spending during the next several years will remain below the symbolically important level of 1 percent of the GNP, overall defense expenditures between 1971 and 1976 are to reach $14.4 billion, with the defense purchasing power of the dollar somewhat higher in the Japanese context than in the corresponding U.S. setting.† The new five-year financial program involves a 220 percent increase over the preceding five years.

* In all fairness, it should be noted that, with the Korean War creating an imminent threat, the SDF was initiated under U.S. guidance, and it was normal for the United States to wish to create at that time essentially a replica of its own defense establishment. It was then also quite normal for the Japanese to emulate American military organization.

† Moreover, there are some grounds for suspecting that not all of the other outlays for research and development or for atomic energy are unrelated to defense. The new program calls for adding 76 F-4 Phantom jet fighters to the air force and the purchase of 920 new planes, bringing the total to 1,740. It also calls for the construction of 14 high-speed missile carriers and 61 other naval craft. This would increase the number of Japanese air vessels to 200. The number of tanks is to be increased to 990.

It should be emphasized that the above, though impressive, does not involve a crash program. But it does involve a steady, measured, and determined effort, pointing step by step toward the emergence of a sizable military capability. It is accompanied also by symbolically subtle and psychologically revealing changes: on Nakasone's urging, the officially used designation of Japan as a "nonnuclear middle-ranked nation" has been changed into "nonnuclear defensive nation," with the reference to Japan's being a middle-ranked nation eliminated; the peace dove with outspread wings, which was part of the coat of arms worn as a shield on the caps of the SDF officers and men, has quietly been excised; a more dashing new uniform has been introduced, replacing the previous one, which was largely a copy of the American.

The return of Okinawa to Japan will further accelerate matters, compelling the Japanese to develop their own concept of defense. The Japanese SDF will be stationed for the first time since World War II outside of the immediate chain of the principal home islands, and this will compel novel and broader defense thinking. In turn, defense issues are likely to become a matter for more intense domestic discussion, thereby eventually acclimatizing the Japanese to the idea that the defense of Japan is, at least in the first instance, a Japanese responsibility. As Nakasone once put it in an interview, "My mission is to open the door on defense discussions and make defense issues so clear that even taxi-drivers and maids will be able to understand and support our defense efforts."[1]

PRESSURES FOR REARMAMENT

Broadly speaking, pressures for Japan to become a major military power can be seen as originating from four sources: feelings of insecurity, concerned economic interests, rising nationalism, and increased uncertainty about the United States.

The insecurity, in part already discussed, focuses directly on

Russia and, to a lesser extent, on China. The Japanese, especially the military, tend to think of South Korea as a necessary defense buffer, hopefully secure under U.S. protection but potentially also a Japanese defense responsibility (a prospect that makes the South Koreans, fearful of an invasion from the north but with still-fresh memories of the fifty-year occupation by invaders from across the sea to the south, extremely jittery). Some officials talk in similar terms in regard to Taiwan, in spite of the widespread Japanese desire for better relations with China. Favorable circumstances permitting, the inclusion of Taiwan into a Japanese defense sphere would be quite tempting, especially to the Japanese military.

Beyond immediate and obvious threats to Japanese security, concern is gradually emerging over the question of how to protect the growing Japanese overseas interests. Many Japanese point to the Straits of Malacca, through which pass the overwhelming portion of Japanese oil supplies (and interruption in the flow of which would simply paralyze Japan), as a point of great vulnerability and hence of justified Japanese defense concern. Some Japanese, particularly leaders of industry, have accordingly argued in favor of naval forces with a long-distance strike and convoy capability.*

Although open advocacy by industrial leaders of rapid and massive rearmament has lately become somewhat more muted, there seems to be among them a fairly widespread inclination to increase the percentage of GNP committed to defense from approximately 1 percent (which has become a kind of symbolic "peace barrier") to somewhere around 3 percent. A prominent Japanese international affairs expert, reputedly connected with

* For example, the influential head of the powerful Keizai Doyuki, Kazutaka Kikawada, has urged that Japan replace Great Britain as the safeguarder of the Straits of Malacca, while Taizo Ishisaka, chairman emeritus of Keidanren, has spoken openly about Japan's need for nuclear arms (Yuichiro Noguchi, "From Economic Superpower to Political Superpower: What the Business-Financial Circles Expect for the 1970s," *Sekai,* January, 1970).

the industrial circles, made a somewhat similar case directly to the Americans, writing in *Foreign Affairs*:

> In light of the fact that nearly all advanced nations of Europe and America expend more than 4% of GNP on national defense, a rate of 2% is certainly reasonable. . . . With most of the advanced Western nations spending well over 4% of their GNP for defense, Japan's expenditures of close to 3.5% on defense and aid together would certainly not be an excessive outlay for the sake of their own peace and prosperity.[2]

His arguments were clearly a mixture of advocacy and prediction.

The appearance of an armaments sector in Japanese industry is doubtless bound to spur such efforts. An organization called the Japanese Weapons Industry Organization has been in existence for several years, and its plenums have been devoted to the advocacy of greater domestic production of arms, both for internal consumption and for export. High industrial officials concerned with the defense sector make no secret in private conversations of their desire to push the scale of SDF reliance on domestically produced armaments up to about 80 percent by 1975 from its present level of approximately 50 percent. They also advocate that a larger share of the budget of the Ministry of Science and Technology be allocated to defense needs.* Official circles concerned with defense have also favored increased SDF reliance on indigenously produced arms, seeing in that a spur to the accumulation of technique and know-how, thus enhancing national power (a point made explicitly by Nakasone in regard to the Japanese decision to produce its own early

* The Keidanren has a special committee concerned with armament production. The minister in charge of science and technology, Wataru Hiraizumi, a youngish man, makes no secret of his view that Japan should become a major power *in all respects*. A close friend of the late Mishima, Hiraizumi impressed me as one of the most articulate Japanese nationalists that I met during my stay in Japan. In any case, his own proclivities aside, the official research budget for defense has been increased from ¥49 billion during the third defense plan to ¥175 billion during the fourth defense plan, a growth of almost 400 percent.

warning aircraft [AEW]). Commenting on the greater emphasis in the fourth defense plan (1972–76) on domestic production, one Japanese industrialist observed, with an obvious touch of satisfaction, "I feel that the seeds sown under the third defense plan put forth buds and have blossomed."[3]

For some industrialists, higher defense production and the export of weapons also provides a hedge against an economic slowdown. The Japanese have already begun to export weapons, though presently these exports are limited to countries that are not involved in disputes, are not Communist nations, and are not countries to which the U.N. has banned the export of weapons.[4] In spite of these restrictions, the industrial circles appear to expect major increases in arms exports, though not much is said about this openly.

It is probably impossible to separate neatly motives derived from insecurity, from economic interests, or from nationalist feelings. Nonetheless, it is evident that higher defense expenditures are publicly favored by those politicians—still a minority—who have been most openly nationalistic, advocating a proud and powerful Japan, arguing that economic power must be accompanied by military power. The new minister of science and technology, Wataru Hiraizumi, a strong nationalist (see footnote page 99), is neither isolated nor atypical; another outstanding example of this outlook is provided by an exceptionally gifted playwright-politician, Shintaro Ishihara, currently a member of the House of Councillors and likely to run for the Diet in the next elections. Ishihara has openly campaigned on behalf of a Japanese nuclear deterrent, and he has generally identified himself with the nationalist cause. Nationalism, quite understandably, is also quite strong within the military establishment, and Japan's relative military standing (particularly its nonnuclear status) is obviously a touchy subject.*

* I gave a lecture at the Japanese Defense Academy, and in that lecture I touched marginally on the need of the defense forces of non-

Uncertainty about the United States serves to reinforce the pressures mentioned above. There is no doubt that advocacy of smaller defense expenditures and fewer defense commitments by a growing number of American politicians is having the effect of strengthening the Japanese inclination to develop an increasingly autonomous defense posture, eventually including a nuclear capability. Japanese security for the last twenty years has rested on the credibility of American protection, that protection being all the more credible since the United States was the undisputed number one global military power. A relative decline toward greater symmetry with the Soviet Union and the simultaneous appearance of profound divisions within the United States, particularly with regard to defense matters, is spurring the Japanese to develop a major military establishment of their own. It is almost axiomatic that an isolationist United States will definitely create a nationalist and militarist Japan.

There is, moreover, an element of self-fulfilling prophecy in the Japanese expectation that their dependence on the United States will decrease. By and large, though uncertainty about the United States produces anxieties, there is also widespread desire to terminate the visible evidences of Japanese dependence on the United States, particularly insofar as U.S. military presence on Japanese soil is concerned. (For example, one top Japanese political leader complained to me—quite rightly, it seems to me—of the symbolic impropriety of American troops being stationed near the Japanese capital.) Even highly pro-United States analysts and politicians, otherwise quite concerned with Japan's security, are in agreement concerning the desirability of terminating the U.S. military presence in Japan.

---

nuclear powers to be concerned with domestic stability. In their written comments on my lecture, which I deliberately solicited in order to obtain a feedback on some of the broader themes raised by me, some of the participants objected to that analysis, suggesting that it reflected "egoism and pride of the U.S. as a nuclear superpower."

In late 1970 a group of Japan's leading defense thinkers, organized since early 1970 in the Security Problem Research Council, issued a document that analyzed U.S.-Japanese defense relations on the assumption that the alliance relationship in the future will not involve the full-time stationing of U.S. forces in Japan. That this was not a matter only of prediction was revealed by the observation to the effect that "readjustment and reduction of bases shall be aimed at a situation where there shall be no constant stationing of the U.S. forces. Unless there is a sudden change in the international situation, early realization of this aim should be promoted continuously and systematically, in consideration of the security of Japan." Attainment of that goal in turn will open "a way to a new treaty in conformity with the new reality at that time." Such a treaty would involve a more even relationship, based on the concept of "emergency cooperation," something that on the Japanese side would quite clearly require a far greater defense effort than currently projected.

OBSTACLES TO REARMAMENT

It would be premature, however, to conclude that Japan is inexorably committed to large-scale rearmament, including nuclear arms. The pressures on behalf of such a commitment, noted above, are countervailed by opposite tendencies, and the outcome of the clash between them may not be decided entirely on home terrain but by broader international developments. Broadly speaking, four principal obstacles can be identified: domestic political considerations, economic constraints, regional considerations, and American sensitivity.

A significant portion of the Japanese electorate is still against large-scale rearmament, and the mass media are allied with the voters. Any overt move by the Japanese government pointing toward the still more rapid acquisition of military power—not to speak of nuclear weapons—provokes strong resistance. The weakening of the LDP hold on the Japanese body politic will make it even more difficult to continue increasing military allocations. Any effort to go nuclear would precipitate massive popular resistance and could split the country politically. Such a move could be undertaken only in a situation in which the sense of national insecurity became overriding.

Economic uncertainties are also a potential impediment. To be sure, some interests have been advocating rearmament as a hedge against recessional tendencies, but an economic squeeze could generally sharpen social divisions, and therefore heighten the residual unpopularity of rearmament. The Finance Ministry gave every impression of already being skeptical about the size of the fourth defense plan, and Fukuda (the finance minister until July 1971 and since then the foreign minister) publicly indicated that in the ministry's judgment the plan involved too rapid a growth rate in defense expenditures, in excess of the projected overall national economic growth rate (18.8 percent per annum over 10.6 percent per annum).[5] The Finance Ministry also expressed a preference for the importation of foreign weapons over domestic production, again on fiscal grounds. The worsening labor supply crisis, moreover, means that it will be both more difficult and more costly for the SDF to compete for the shrinking number of males of military age, with some military planners saying that by 1975 a 20 percent cut in SDF manpower will become inevitable.

Fear of arousing external sensitivities is likely to prove even more important. The Japanese, as noted, are extremely alert to foreign reactions, and their economic success makes them doubly anxious to cultivate a positive image. The Japanese are aware that their Asian neighbors still fear them and that a massively rearmed Japan would generate anxieties and hostilities that, by themselves, would almost offset any additional element of national security thereby gained. It is therefore one thing quietly to enlarge Japanese military forces, quietly to increase the sale of Japanese arms, quietly to train Indonesian and other Asian military personnel, but quite another for Japan to surface as a major military power.

These considerations apply also, although in a somewhat different way, to Japanese relations with her Communist neighbors. Though both China and the Soviet Union are the principal threats to Japanese security, many Japanese feel that a steady and patient effort to improve relations with both powers, while retaining a strong link with the United States, is the more rational way of enhancing Japanese security. Hence, short of a major aggravation in relations with either Peking or Moscow, the anticipated hostile Soviet or Chinese reaction to major Japanese defense programs will also represent a significant impediment on the road to national military power.

Much the same set of considerations, though cast in a different set of values, applies to the Japanese-U.S. relationship. Here, the stake would be existing friendship. Many Japanese, as already noted, are concerned over the credibility of America's security guarantees. At the same time they are anxious not to translate that anxiety into a self-fulfilling prophecy, and they suspect that a remilitarizing Japan could not only not count on American friendship but might even stimulate American enmity. The problem here, therefore, is one of striking a balance: the Americans clearly favor some further assumption by Japan of defense responsibilities in the Pacific; many Japanese desire such enlargement, yet many also fear its longer-term consequences for the American-Japanese relationship. Minor and cautious steps, not major leaps forward, are the only proper prescription.

It follows, on balance, that the most probable pattern for the Japanese security program will be a continuation of its deliberately prudent and even somewhat covert buildup, but at a pace that, if maintained, would not make Japan by 1975 into a major military power. It will give Japan, however, the necessary jump-off position either for a quick but massive rearmament program or for continued measured growth.

THE YEAR OF DECISION

Indeed, it does appear that 1975 will become the crucial year of decision, a year in which the die may be cast. The Japanese expect that by 1975 most American forces will be out of Japan, and it may also be expected that the Japanese will quietly press for the removal of most American bases by that date. Joint base use and rapid U.S. deployment in the event of a crisis will be the officially favored alternatives, but once the United States is out a new military situation will have automatically arisen. A novel degree of self-sufficiency will become, almost by definition, a necessity.

In keeping with this, the Japanese will have to move forward with the development of a Japanese security doctrine. In 1970 the then head of the Japanese SDF, Nakasone, defined that emerging concept with the suggestive phrase that Japan "can be viewed as a rabbit with long ears plus the defenses of a porcupine," i.e., a sophisticated intelligence network (both technetronic and otherwise), combined with efficient home island defense forces, to make external aggression too costly. In keeping with the former objective, the Japanese have already been assuming many of the American intelligence-gathering activities in the northern Pacific area, including highly sophisticated tracking of Soviet military satellites, Soviet and Chinese missile firings, and electronic eavesdropping. (According to published accounts, most of that activity is centered in Chitose, Hokkaido, a former NSA establishment taken over by the Japanese SDF.) However, defining what it takes to make Japan into a "porcupine" is much more difficult, and this is where the search for a strategic doctrine comes in. Even the Japanese press has called for it, urging a comprehensive effort to relate Japan's economic-diplomatic objective to Japan's security requirements.* The setting up of a Japanese strategic research institute has also been recommended and is apparently under consideration.†

In general, given both technological developments and the sharpening labor shortage, more emphasis in Japanese defense efforts is likely to be put on technology and science, more stress on mobility (e.g., from tanks to helicopters), and probably also on increasing the range of Japanese striking power (especially given the assumption of responsibility for Okinawa). This in turn will give rise to the ticklish question of what actually constitutes the legitimate defense perimeter of Japan.‡

In this regard, it seems quite likely that the years ahead will see growing defense cooperation between Japan, Australia, and even possibly Indonesia. A maritime triangle based on these three insular constellations would make a great deal of sense: their strategic needs (essentially maritime and airspace) mesh; their economies (one advanced industrial, one semi-industrial and extracting, one preindustrial but rich in raw materials) complement one another; their potential enemies (either Soviet naval

* "Is it now not the time when, including all these diplomatic policies, a state strategy based on a long-range view should be seriously studied? It can be said that people will hardly be able to understand the Fourth Defense Plan and revision of the Status of Forces agreement, until such a state strategy is formed" (*Yomiuri Shimbun,* January 9, 1971).

† The lead in this has been taken by the prominent and very thoughtful Japanese scholar of international affairs, Masamichi Inoki, who is currently serving as commandant of the Japanese Defense Academy.

‡ The Koreans were rather offended by the inclusion of South Korea in the Nixon-Sato communique of 1970 as part of Japan's defense perimeter. The Japanese concern with Korea is historically rooted. "Thus in a document of 1890, Yamagata Aritomo set out his views on national policy by distinguishing between Japan's line of sovereignty (*shukensen*) and line of interest or advantage (*riekisen*). The latter, he argued, was essential to the former if Japan was to become truly independent of reliance on outside help. And Korea was Japan's line of advantage. Its independence was essential to Japan. . . ." (Nobutake Ike, "War and Modernization," in Robert E. Ward, ed., *Political Development in Modern Japan* [Princeton, N.J.: Princeton University Press, 1968], p. 182.)

threat in the Indian Ocean or Chinese pressure) are the same. The emergence of such a Pacific maritime triangle will be gradual, for security cooperation with the Japanese will have to overcome strong political obstacles within Indonesia and Australia. Nonetheless, movement in this direction seems likely. It would provide a logical framework for a relevant Japanese defense posture, less politically threatening than implied by the more forward defense perimeter based on Taiwan and Korea. The maritime triangle would not be incompatible with more normal relations with China; the forward defense perimeter might well be, and would have to be premised on continued and somewhat aggressive Chinese hostility.

For the time being, however, problems of overt strategy and weapons development are likely to be handled with a caution verging on disingenuousness. Indeed, that is precisely what some leading and perceptive Japanese strategic thinkers have been recommending. They have warned against an overly active policy that might draw hostile and suspicious attention from Asian countries, and have urged that, for the time being, Japan should put emphasis on the economic sector of aid or cooperation. Later, she can look for an effective way of promoting cooperation in political spheres. As to its military contribution, it will be prudent not to change Japan's present low posture until Japan becomes confident of its necessity and positive effect.[6]

Thus, by 1975 Japan will be ready and will expect a redefinition of its military alliance with the United States. Given existing trends and commitments, the basic option by then will be either armed neutrality (autonomous defense and autonomous foreign policy) or some new, more equal relationship with the United States. Moreover, by 1975 Japan will have inched up to a point when it will be ready to confront the fundamental defense question: Should it go nuclear?

PROTONUCLEAR POSTURE

That by 1975 Japan will be in a protonuclear posture seems to be clear. Japan succeeded not long ago in the centrifugal separation method for the production of uranium 235, making the separation at a low cost at relatively small plants.[7] Similarly, Japan is making rapid strides in the assimilation of nuclear energy. By around 1985 Japan will be producing approximately 30 to 40 million kilowatts of electric power and will have a sufficient supply of plutonium, enough to manufacture several hundred atomic bombs a year, if needed. There is general consensus among experts that Japan could even now quickly shift into weapons production, but it would still take a relatively long period of time (about the rest of the decade) for Japan to acquire a respectable nuclear deterrent, given its lack of competence in weapons technology and relevant data.*

By 1975 this critical time period (during which Japan would be subjected to maximum external and internal pressures) could be cut to about five years at most; by 1980 it could be shrunk further, to under three years. All of this is based on the assumption that the United States would neither actively support nor actively obstruct such a Japanese nuclear weapons program.†

? Moreover, the public allergy to nuclear weapons seems to be over. Though most Japanese still do not favor them, many are resigned to them and expect—some perhaps secretly wish—

* Though definitions may vary, it could perhaps be asserted that a respectable nuclear deterrent for Japan would mean roughly ten nuclear Poseidon-type submarines, with approximately 60 percent of them operational at all times. (U.S. operational level is approximately 30 percent, but that appears considerably less than the Soviets are maintaining, and the Japanese could certainly maintain a higher degree of operational efficiency.)

† The Japanese defense planners have apparently considered under what circumstances the United States might actually provide nuclear assistance to the Japanese nuclear program, and their conclusion was that such assistance was extremely unlikely.

Japan to acquire them. This is borne out by a large variety of public opinion polls, which seem to indicate a widespread expectation of Japan acquiring nuclear weapons, even though those favoring such nuclear weapons are still in the minority. Symptomatically, younger people indicate a higher expectation of Japan going nuclear than older people. There has also been no outpouring of popular demand for the ratification by Japan of the Nuclear Nonproliferation Treaty (NPT), while the top LDP political leaders have shifted from a categorical rejection of nuclear weapons to a highly contingent one. Nakasone has thus spoken rather casually of Japan at some point building nuclear submarines, while a very top Japanese leader said to me that Japan will not go nuclear unless the international situation made it necessary for it to do so.*

However, it is important to realize that there is an enormous gap between an abstract resignation, inclination, or even the desire to go nuclear and the actual implementation of the decision to become a nuclear power. Even if Japan keeps inching up to a nuclear posture, and even though the difficult implementation stage can thereby be telescoped, there will still remain the several critical years during which the decision will have to be executed. These years would be extraordinarily difficult for the Japanese government and polity. The decision could precipitate a great deal of international outcry and domestic opposition, and jeopardize many of Japan's vital ties.

It is, hence, not likely to be undertaken short of a major international crisis. Moreover, even then it is likely that the Japanese government will strive to dilute the drama of such a decision by indirect, maybe even surreptitious, arrangements with a sympathetic power, such as Australia. A joint Australian-Japanese nuclear program or, even better, an Australian one on

* There have also been some reports that the Japanese Air Force has been running simulated nuclear attacks as part of its training exercises, although without "official" orders to that effect from the top.

Japan's behalf would be attractive.[8] But anything of this sort would have to be preceded by some jolting experience, shattering Japanese reliance on the United States and inducing a willingness at some point even to provoke American opposition. A precipitous American disengagement from some area, achieved under either Chinese or Soviet nuclear threat, could be one such eventuality. A dramatic cut in U.S. defense programs and a dramatic turn within the United States toward left-wing isolationism might be another. Either one can galvanize in Japan irresistible feelings of insecurity, prompting one of those dramatic switches in behavior already noted in Japanese history.

The question whether Japan opts for autonomous defense, including even nuclear weaponry, or for some other security posture thus turns ultimately on the shape of the U.S.-Japanese relationship. The next several years are likely to be decisive in that respect. But any redefinition of that relationship will also have to take into account the intangible element of Japan's quest for status. That quest, though by itself insufficient to push Japan to extreme measures, is an important element on the scales, one that certainly predisposes many Japanese toward the more assertive and autonomous policy in the area of military power. Considerations of security and of status therefore represent critical elements in the changing pattern of American-Japanese relations.

6

The Relationship with the United States

IT IS NOW CUSTOMARY for both the Americans and the Japanese to reiterate on every major occasion the overriding importance of the ties binding America and Japan. There is much talk of partnership, of close consultations, of common interests, and of friendship. Yet for a close relationship between two major powers—which the American-Japanese relationship undoubtedly is—there are disturbing imbalances in it, imbalances that portend some difficult years ahead. In its essence, politically and even more psychologically, American-Japanese ties are more important to the Japanese than to the Americans, and this the Japanese sense and resent; economically, the relationship now favors the Japanese, and this the Americans increasingly begrudge. The interaction of the two makes for trouble, unless major adjustments are made on each side.

For many years, America has been both Japan's roof against

rain and its window on the world. The present Japanese elite has become accustomed to relating itself to the world via America, and to taking foreign events into account by first calculating their impact on America and on American-Japanese relations. Symptomatic of this was the enormous emphasis placed in the Japanese Foreign Ministry (and also in leading businesses) on training an elite attuned to American ways of doing things. For a diplomat, the crowning of his career, after attaining the post of vice minister of foreign affairs, was to be accredited ambassador to Washington. All this has stood in sharp contrast to the American attitude, which, while respecting Japan, put prior and higher emphasis on European and Soviet matters. Japan, on the American side, has been a matter of concern for Asian specialists, but not for "generalists" broadly concerned with international affairs (who, typically, were actually European specialists).*

The sudden emergence of Japan as an economic power enjoying a massive surplus in trade with the United States, the success of Japanese industry in competing with American products, and the simultaneous difficulties confronting America as it shouldered alone, for better or for worse, the various cold war legacies, all shook American complacency and have caused Americans to reassess their relations with Japan. As a result, on both sides of the Pacific, new attention is now being focused on the American-Japanese relationship.

This attention notwithstanding, the basic reality still remains unchanged: for Japan, the American-Japanese relationship is the crucial variable in its foreign policy. Japan's postwar recovery hinged on close ties with America, and its foreign policy has been woven around the American-Japanese relationship. Japanese postwar reconstruction involved a concerted effort to model many Japanese institutions and practices on the U.S. model,

* This, incidentally, was one of the key reasons why I decided to devote a year to becoming better acquainted with Japan.

repeating in a different context and with different substance the post-Meiji restoration effort to remodel Japanese society on the West European example. It is precisely this very centrality of the relationship that poses the danger of a Japanese overreaction to strains in American-Japanese relations.

A SUDDEN RUPTURE?

This has happened before. American-Japanese relations were friendly until Japan began to emerge as a great power after 1905. The American attitude toward the Japanese changed markedly thereafter, and the United States began to block and obstruct Japan's quest for great-power status and for preeminence in Asia. (At the same time, America's racial discrimination against Japanese immigrants compelled the Japanese to accept "voluntary restraints"—then called a "gentlemen's agreement"—designed to stem the flow of immigrants to the United States.) At one point, U.S. diplomatic maneuvers even prompted a brief period of Japanese-Russian cooperation.* Some Japanese wonder whether history is not about to repeat itself. The United States is again anxious, and U.S. pressures for "voluntary restraint," this time in economics, are suspected to have been reinforced by U.S. racial feelings.† At the same time, uncertainty about U.S. intentions in the Pacific makes Japan a tempting target for Soviet diplomacy, even though more Japanese would be tempted by the lure of a grand Asian alliance, linking China and Japan, than by closer cooperation with the disliked and distrusted Russians.

All this makes for an uncertain mood among the Japanese in

* The specific event involved was the Knox Neutralization Plan for Manchuria.

† Racial sensitivity also appears to be at the roots of the Japanese resentment of the U.S. policy in Vietnam. To many Japanese, "the war is unpopular because it seems to the Japanese that the strong white man is tormenting the weak Asians" (*Asahi Shimbun,* July 10, 1971).

regard to the United States. The United States still enjoys enormous popularity, especially among the masses. A visitor is struck by this over and over again, especially when traveling throughout the Japanese islands. All public opinion polls demonstrate Japanese goodwill for the United States and the widespread popular recognition of Japanese self-interest in close cooperative ties with the United States. But within the elite a change is taking place, a change toward a more critical and in some cases even antipathetic attitude. This is not only a matter of the intellectuals and the students, some of whom have been calling for a more critical Japanese approach in Japanese studies of America and among whom the self-flagellations of American intellectuals find an eager and receptive audience; it is felt also in the upper echelons of the governmental-business elite. For example, the Foreign Ministry is coming under sustained criticism as "the Asian Department of the United States State Department" for being excessively deferential to U.S. interests (while MITI is just as often praised for its properly pro-Japanese posture).[1] Similar sentiments have been voiced semiprivately by some of the top LDP contenders for power, in itself a symptom of the changing Japanese attitude.

The abruptness and the secrecy of President Nixon's initiative in the summer of 1971 toward China further intensified the resentment among the upper levels of the Japanese elite. There was bitterness against U.S. deception, especially since for the preceding six months the United States had been assuring the Japanese that there was no U.S.-Japanese race to Peking and had been urging the Japanese to join in an effort to concert U.S. and Japanese policies toward China (with high-level consultations to that end actually held). The Japanese felt deceived, outmaneuvered, and embarrassed. All of a sudden, the U.S.-Japanese "partnership" began to look very hollow, and very many Japanese concluded that the United States had never really meant what it had said. Anxieties that the United States was opting for China over Japan were mixed with resentment over what was regarded as rather disloyal U.S. behavior.

Japanese uncertainty about the United States was intensified by conflicting U.S. signals as to the real meaning of the Nixon doctrine and by the rather widespread view among upper-level Japanese that the United States was losing its taste for world leadership.* For many Japanese the Nixon doctrine signifies a general withdrawal from Asia, caused more basically by a case of national fatigue.[2] yes

This shift in elite attitudes could not fail to affect broader popular attitudes, and a new popular mood toward the United States is gradually emerging. It is more critical, less inclined to idealize all that is American, somewhat more prone to emphasize the negatives. In part, it is the outcome of Japan's own economic recovery: there is no longer quite the same need to envy and admire America's material attainments. But it is more than that: the change, encouraged by a much more critical attitude toward the United States in the Japanese mass media (which in turn reflects predominant attitudes of the intellectual community), is also caused by a rising sense of national pride. Given the international realities of Japan in the last two decades, rising national pride has no alternative but to assert itself in the first instance *against* the United States.

However, it would be wrong to conclude that the Japanese public is becoming anti-American. As asserted earlier, the dominant attitude is still by far pro-American and, in my judgment, is likely to remain so for the foreseeable future. The interdependence of Japanese-American interests in Asia is generally

* Though my own enthusiasm for the Nixon doctrine is under rather firm control (see my "Half Past Nixon," *Foreign Policy,* no. 3 [Summer 1971]), I spent a fair amount of time while in Japan attempting to explain that it was a misunderstanding to view the Nixon doctrine simply as a symptom of U.S. isolationism (e.g., "The New Dimension in American Foreign Policy," *Nihon Keizai Kenkyu Senta,* Kaiho, no. 148 [Japan Economic Research Center Report no. 148], Tokyo, March 15, 1971).

recognized, and Japanese dependence on the United States—while naturally resented by some—is viewed as a fact of life. What is new is the more critical, more assertive mood, and the possibility of a sudden emotional upsurge in the event of a major crisis in American-Japanese relations. The public mood could then turn strongly anti-United States, not because of an enduring and widespread anti-Americanism but because of feelings of betrayal and disappointment—as well as injured pride and some underlying resentment.

These highly complex and volatile feelings—which, to repeat, it would be grossly oversimplifying to label as anti-American—could surface particularly quickly if American-Japanese disagreements adversely affected Japan's economic well-being. A recession within Japan would be blamed by many Japanese, right or wrong, on America. Given the "metastable" interdependence between Japanese economic and sociopolitical order, an economic squeeze within Japan, especially if produced in part by external, particularly American, pressures, would almost certainly precipitate a turmoil both in Japanese political life and in Japanese-American relations. At that stage, Japan might react desperately, either by undertaking a crash program of military development, in total disregard of public reactions at home and abroad, or by adopting a new foreign orientation more openly critical of the United States and more inclined to explore the possibility of Japanese-Chinese diplomatic-economic cooperation.

Of these two somewhat remote possibilities, the latter is more probable. As noted earlier, a program of accelerated large-scale rearmament is more likely to be induced by international developments, particularly by a combination of continued American disengagement with some critical precipitating event. The consequences of an economic crisis within Japan would be as divisive politically as they would be anti-American internationally. Hence a consensus for a crash program of military development would be more difficult to obtain than agreement on what—in the back of their heads—even many right-wing, as well as left-wing, Japanese desire: some sort of grand alliance with China. In a situation of real domestic crisis and external rupture with America, the Chinese option would be emotionally the more attractive response for a great many Japanese, in spite of all the concrete obstacles already outlined earlier.

The issue of China could suddenly divide America and Japan in still another way. As noted, the Nixon initiative toward Peking violated the spirit, if not the letter, of the principle of joint consultation, and it is quite likely that in the future it will be more difficult for the two capitals to concert their policies. The Japanese henceforth will feel even more justified than they are anyway to follow their own interests in such matters as Taiwan or the establishment of direct diplomatic relations with Peking.

It is, therefore, not unrealistic to conjure up the following scenario: Japan and China have diplomatic relations; China is in the United Nations and in the Security Council; the United States, despite the Nixon initiative, has still only indirect ties with Peking and it is still tied by the security treaty with Taiwan. A military crisis in the Taiwan Strait could then have the effect of pitting Japan diplomatically, in the U.N. and elsewhere, *against* the United States and on the side of China. For the first time since World War II, Japan and the United States would be adversaries.

Such reversal of alliances (whether because of economics or because of China), however, is the extreme possibility, and it is still unlikely. As argued earlier, enduring Japanese-Chinese collaboration would require more than just a tactical shift in the orientation of the Japanese ruling circles. It would go counter to the broader financial and economic involvements of Japan and to the widespread popular support for continued Japanese-American ties. A fundamental reversal would require the simultaneous conjunction of an emotional and political crisis in relations with the United States with a political upheaval within the LDP or in the LDP's national position with an economic crisis within Japan. Nonetheless, it is important to mention it, because—though the probabilities of such a denouement are low—both the Americans and the Japanese should ponder the imponderable. Indeed, the Chinese option could find some adherents on the American side as well, and America and Japan could suddenly find that what is now a specter for each has inadvertently become a reality for both.

A LINGERING CRISIS

A progressive deterioration in the American-Japanese relationship could eventually also create a crisis, with similar temptations. Such a lingering crisis is certainly more probable; indeed, it could be argued that the Japanese-American relationship is already experiencing it. It involves basically three broad issues: economics, security, and status.

The economic issue has already surfaced, and both sides are, at least, aware of it. The Japanese business community has finally come to realize that the post-World War II attitude toward Japan, which deliberately favored the Japanese recovery, cannot be maintained in a setting of greater economic symmetry. This realization has been belated and grudging, and it is still hesitant. To the extent that they can, the Japanese will strive to minimize their concessions; they will wage a rearguard action on the yen, conceding eventually but only when the world monetary system is on the eve of a broad crisis, and they will liberalize their economy while striving still to exclude some of the more sensitive items (e.g., computers). It is unlikely that they will abandon their limitations on foreign ownership.

They will resist and concede for the same reason: Japanese-American trade is more important to Japan than to the United States.* On the one hand, this condition makes the Japanese

* "In the case of Japan, exports accounted for 9.1% of the GNP (the average for the period 1965–68), of which 2.9% was exports to the United States. In the case of America, its exports account for only 4%

reluctant to abandon their advantageous position because they feel themselves more vulnerable; on the other hand, eventually they will because—to put it quite bluntly—they have no option but to do so. But the concessions, slow and grudging, will probably not alter, at least in the near future, the basically favorable position that Japan enjoys in U.S.-Japanese trade. Japanese price indices have favored exports over domestic consumer prices (giving rise to charges of dumping),* and Japan will continue to import primarily raw materials and agricultural products from

---

of the GNP, of which only 0.4% was to Japan. As to the meaning of trade between the two in their respective exports in general, Japan's exports to the U.S. account for 31.5% of all exports, whereas in the case of the U.S., its exports to Japan have less weight, accounting for only 10.2%" (Chikara Makino, "Japan-United States Relations," *Tsusan Journal* 3–4 [1970]). Mr. Makino is in the planning office of MITI.

Similarly, Dr. Saburo Okita calculates that "it may be said that economically Japan is eight times more sensitive than the U.S. in terms of trade between the two countries" ("United States-Japan Economic Relations" [Paper prepared for the Subcommittee on Foreign Economic Policy, Joint Economic Committee, Congress of the United States, 1970, p. 9]).

* EXPORT AND DOMESTIC CONSUMER PRICE INDICES for THE UNITED STATES AND JAPAN (1963=100)

	U.S.		Japan	
Year	*Exp.*	*Dom.*	*Exp.*	*Dom.*
1960	99	96	102	82
1961	101	97	98	87
1962	100	98	98	93
1963	100	100	100	100
1964	101	101	101	104
1965	104	103	101	112
1966	107	106	101	117
1967	110	109	101	122
1968	111	114	102	129
1969	115	120	105	136
1970	122	127	110	146

Source: International Monetary Fund, *International Financial Statistics,* various issues, as cited by Fred J. Borch, chairman of the board, General Electric Company, in his testimony before the Subcommittee on International Trade of the Senate Finance Committee, May 21, 1971.

the United States and export finished, and increasingly sophisticated, goods.

Indeed, if Japanese concessions on liberalization obviate the American case against Japan and reduce the likelihood of American protectionism, it is quite likely that the advantage enjoyed by Japan will even grow further. Computers and a few extremely advanced items aside, U.S. exports to Japan are likely to continue falling behind Japanese exports to the United States. Unless there is a major improvement on the American side (involving higher industrial productivity and competitiveness), or unless Japan is somehow prevailed upon to exercise greater self-restraint (the American case for which would be much weakened by Japanese liberalization), "Japan's exports to the U.S. in 1975 are expected to reach about $11.2 billion, while imports from America will be about $7.8 billion. Still further, in 1980, exports will be about $20.5 billion, and imports about $14.8 billion. Thus, big excesses in exports on the part of Japan are to be expected."[3]

Continued economic friction is therefore likely, even in spite of a reciprocal will to accommodate. The textile crisis could soon be followed by an automobile crisis, with the U.S. industry and labor concerned in a much stronger position to command political support than was even the case with the U.S. textile industry. The American side, so far, has been wasting its political capital to defend its secondary industries, and this has put the United States at a further disadvantage. The United States may, therefore, not find itself in a strong position to bargain on behalf of its more vital economic interest, and much will depend on Japanese good sense. The pressures for Japanese concessions, ultimately giving the Japanese no option but to concede, would thus culminate in a situation that is bound to be most unpleasant for the Americans: a somewhat last-minute Japanese realization that an economic crisis in America would pain Japan as much as it would pain the Americans.

The far-reaching economic measures adopted by the Nixon administration in August 1971 reflected the American desperation concerning the Japanese unwillingness to accommodate. As a result of these measures, the economic relationship may become somewhat more balanced, but at the cost of long-standing U.S. commitments to free trade. Mutual recriminations between the Americans and the Japanese, as well as the possibility of some retaliatory Japanese actions, seem inevitable, even though Japanese unwillingness to heed earlier warnings had much to do with the unilateral character of the American actions.

Security problems are also likely to create lingering strains on the Japanese-American relationship. The return to Japan of Okinawa, and the assumption by the Japanese of the responsibility for the defense of that island, has thrust Japan into a strategic posture for which the country is not yet ready. Militarily, Japan is not prepared to play a strategic role, yet that is implied by the arrival of the Japanese SDF on that geographically key Pacific bastion. Politically, Japan is not ready to play that role either by itself or, as is implied by the present arrangements for Okinawa, in close military cooperation with the U.S. forces. Political tensions and public resentment are the likely outcomes of the complex tactical and strategic arrangements that will still have to be worked out for the joint use of bases and for the joint actions on Okinawa.* The return of Okinawa to Japan has thus tied Japan to the United States more closely than before, and the new links have a political pinch.

* The need for such arrangements is strongly implied by U.S. officials: "As to the use of military bases in Okinawa, Japanese-U.S. cooperation in the form of joint military action accompanied with detailed consultation, would have to be pushed forward. Unless cooperative relations between Japan and the U.S. go smoothly, it would become impossible for the Seventh Fleet or U.S. military bases in Japan and Okinawa to fulfill their security functions for the Republic of Korea, Taiwan, and their peripheral areas" (Robert Osgood, interview in *Asahi Shimbun*, June 27, 1971). Mr. Osgood was a member of Mr. Nixon's National Security Council until 1971.

More generally, the Japanese are somewhat confused by and resent the U.S. efforts to get Japan to assume a larger security role in Asia. "Japanization" of Asian security does not appeal to the majority of the Japanese public nor to much of its business community, nor, for that matter, to most other Asians. Yet, perhaps somewhat unwittingly, the United States has generated the impression that the major objective of the Nixon doctrine is to obtain a larger involvement of Japan in Asian security, in part as compensation for declining U.S. involvement. To be sure, this goal is not altogether unattractive to some Japanese, especially because it satisfies their status aspirations, but, for the moment at least, it does not command majority appeal.

The problem, of course, is further complicated by the fact that the security of Japan proper is inseparable from the wider problem of Asian security, and the American side has a legitimate complaint when it argues that even defense of Japan in the main is still shouldered (and financed) by the United States. Yet a more autonomous self-defense of Japan, less reliant on U.S. protection, inevitably raises broader strategic problems for the region as a whole, including the politically sensitive prospect of the Japanization of Asian security.

The security issue will surface with increasing sharpness during the next several years, with 1975 as the probable crisis point (see Chapter 5, pages 105–107). By then not only will the American-Japanese military relationship be ripe for fundamental review, requiring probably an altogether new alliance structure and strategic concept, but it may be further complicated by the nuclear issue. Should circumstances predispose the Japanese to pursue more actively and more openly the development of their own nuclear weapons, the United States will confront the key choices of either (a) directly assisting the Japanese, (b) indirectly assisting them, (c) not assisting them, (d) obstructing quietly and discreetly, (e) objecting strongly and energetically impeding the Japanese efforts.

Alternatives (c), (d), and (e) would inescapably generate political tension, although each would be of a somewhat different magnitude; alternatives (a) and (b) would require much closer cooperation, strategically and politically, than even currently seems likely. While my own general predisposition on this matter is outlined in the concluding section, it is almost self-evident that the surfacing of the nuclear problem will immensely complicate a relationship that is already becoming more complicated as the U.S. decreases its security role in Asia. On the Japanese side, the assumption of greater responsibility for even the defense of their home islands requires also a broader definition of Japan's role in Asia and in the world, and that, as we have seen, is neither intellectually simple nor devoid of internal political complications.

This brings us to a consideration of the question of status in the Japanese relationship with the United States. This is a matter both of psychology and of actual arrangements. The psychological dimension in the relationship is extremely important, especially on the Japanese side, and both sides have been insensitive to it. The American side has not been fully responsive to the Japanese quest for higher status and to the need to appeal to the more honorable and magnanimous side of the Japanese character when confronted with difficulties in dealing with Japan. Instead, the United States has alternated between a highly paternalistic attitude and blustering threats. The result has been both to undermine the credibility of the argument that the Japanese must make concessions for the sake of good American-Japanese relations and to stimulate Japanese resentments. The following secret telegram might have been sent by the U.S. ambassador to Tokyo early in 1971:

The Ambassador stresses the importance of understanding Japanese psychology, fundamentally unlike that of any Western nation. Japanese reactions to any particular set of circumstances cannot be measured, nor can Japanese actions be predicted by any Western measuring rod. . . . Should the United States expect or await agreement by the Japanese government, in the present preliminary conversations, to clear-cut commitments which would satisfy the United States government both as to principle and as to concreter detail, almost certainly the conversations will drag along indefinitely and unproductively until the Sato cabinet and its supporting elements desiring rapprochement with the United States, will come to the conclusion that the outlook for an agreement is hopeless and that the United States government is only playing for time. . . . This will result in the Sato government's being discredited and in a revulsion of anti-American feelings, and thus may, and probably will, lead to unbridled acts . . .

Actually, the telegram had been sent in early 1941 by the then U.S. ambassador to Tokyo, and only the word "Konoye" had been changed to "Sato."[4]

On their side, the Japanese have been shortsighted and motivated primarily by short-term goals. Also, as a Japanese scholar suggests, in part because of their inferiority complex vis-à-vis the United States, the Japanese side has been excessively rigid.[5] He goes on to point out that "if Japan can take a step further and reach the point where it will think of the other side's position and will seek long-range gains even by offering concessions from a short-range viewpoint, then it can be said that the Japanese have true self-confidence."[6] Similarly, a thoughtful Japanese government official points out that

the Japanese people have an unfortunate tendency to lack international sense, in view of their geographical and historical background, and to wish to settle various international problems according to their own yardstick or principles. They tend to lack the posture of coping with international relations flexibly from a comprehensive standpoint, giving thought to the various complicated factors involved in international relations.[7]

He warns that Japanese nationalism could become emotionally aroused in an anti-American direction if the difficulties between the two sides create the popular impression that America is deliberately obstructing Japan's rise to greater status in the world.

Thus, the Japanese side has failed to win the goodwill that concessions should have generated because, when such concessions are finally made, they are made so gracelessly that they cease to look like concessions and begin to look like extortion—with neither side then happy with the outcome. The American side—having failed to articulate clearly where it stands, oscillating between stealth and threat, neglecting to exploit the elements of honor and sentiment in the Japanese character, slighting Japan on the grand issues of world affairs—is made to look alternatively as if it was almost entirely dependent on Japanese kindness or as if it did not care at all for the Japanese-American relationship.

Given both Japan's dependence on the United States for almost a quarter of a century and this web of emotional complications, the Japanese quest for higher international status thus tends to be deflected into self-assertiveness, potentially even hostility, against the United States. The problem is made more difficult by the fact that Japan wants to be treated and considered like a world power yet does not quite know what it takes to be one, a condition that imposes a special burden on the United States. Since the Japanese have still failed to define for themselves how they envisage a greater world role for Japan, the United States must be extremely careful to avoid pushing Japan into an essentially anti-American definition of that role. There is, as we have repeatedly noted, the potential for a demonstratively anti-American leadership even within the LDP, and American clumsiness and insensitivity could easily have the effect of making it surface.

THE DILEMMA OF THE ONE ALTERNATIVE

Such an eventuality would be especially tragic, since basically neither side wishes a rupture and since both sides, on the rational plane, recognize the desirability of closer cooperation. Indeed, at the risk of certain inconsistency, one can almost say that it is primarily the United States that can turn Japan away from the United States, since Japan will not do it as a matter of rational choice. Short of a dramatic rupture in the context of a sudden crisis, even the lingering tensions will not bring about the divorce, though the relationship may become poisoned by mounting antagonisms.

It thus behooves the United States to make a special effort to create some sort of a framework that can subsume the basic problems that exist and will persist in the Japanese-American relationship. In all likelihod, economic tensions will continue, even though, since both sides have an interest in such contrivance, accommodation will be contrived. Security problems will persist, not only because both powers will confront changes in their military relations with each other, but also because the Pacific region will continue to present dangers and uncertainties. Psychological and status problems will beset the American-Japanese relationship, especially if Japan increasingly—and inevitably—moves into a more active political posture internationally.

It is unlikely that any of these problems can be altogether resolved, for the reality of any complex international relationship is that it involves problems. The Japanese-American relationship cannot be free of tension, even under the best of circumstances. What is increasingly apparent, however, is that, to minimize some of the problems confronting Japan and America, a broader approach will be necessary. Neither economics nor security nor status are matters that can be handled any longer exclusively in a bilateral framework. Each of the above involves issues that spill over into a wider international plane. Hence, as will be argued more fully in the next section, both Tokyo and Washington in the years ahead will have to fortify their relationship—if that relationship is to remain a constructive one and if a balance is to be struck between the economic and political asymmetries noted at the outset—by relating it to a wider framework of international cooperation.

Conclusions and Recommendations

BROADLY SPEAKING, the Japan that emerges from this report is a country in the midst of wide change, and the process of that change, as it accelerates, could become increasingly disruptive. Socially, Japan is moving from traditionalism to modernity; politically, from a representative democratic system, superimposed on a rather feudal pattern of authority and cliquism, to a more direct populist relationship between the leader and the masses, with more stress on personalist politics; in values, from a single-faceted concentration on a common goal, reinforced by self-denying discipline, to a more complex and even conflicting set of objectives, involving both greater emphasis on national pride and on social good; internationally, from a posture of dependence to self-assertiveness.

Moreover, almost everything that is impacting on Japan from

the outside is working to weaken the forces that have traditionally given Japan its cohesion. Increasing international involvement and communication are diluting established loyalties, stimulating growing hedonism, changing Japanese political style. Japanese social resilience is high and, therefore, many of these external influences are diluted or absorbed, but an overload of the new within the old is gradually developing, and sudden breakthroughs are to be expected. It is this which gives Japan its quality of metastability.

A further general point before listing in a more specific and summary fashion our conclusions: since the trauma of its confrontation with the outside world little over a century ago, much of Japanese behavior has been shaped by the necessity of responding to that outside world. This is not to suggest a kind of automatic external determinism to Japanese behavior—for obviously the traditions of Japanese culture, the energy of its people, and the structure of Japanese society were crucial givens in the overall conduct of the Japanese—but it is to argue that these were galvanized and pushed in a particular direction by the nature of the outside impulses and challenges. Japanese pre–World War II policy was very much shaped by the Japanese imitation of Western imperialism and nationalism, and by the rigidity of the American attitude toward Japan; Japan's postwar history was nurtured by the United States; Japanese behavior in the seventies is likely to be very much influenced by how the Japanese interpret the United States and its global behavior.

To be sure, all countries are influenced by others, but of the major nations in the world Japan seems more vulnerable to external inputs, more affected in its internal and external conduct by outside impulses. It is this susceptibility to external stimuli, as well as its extremely limited and exposed geopolitical position, that compels some qualification to the increasingly widespread view of Japan as a superpower. In some respects, particularly in terms of its national energy and economic power, it certainly is that, and it could become one militarily as well. And yet in terms of true inner confidence, a secure sense of one's own position in the world, of a pattern of constancy in internal and external behavior—as well as simply in terms of directly controlled material assets (including such obvious ones as territory)—Japan suffers from major handicaps, from high vulnerability. In brief, lacking subjective and objective self-sufficiency, its economic attainments and even its prospective military power are a fragile blossom.

With these three general conclusions in mind: (1) social metastability, (2) high susceptibility to external stimuli, (3) fragility of its position, let us now recapitulate very briefly also our more specific conclusions and then develop some recommendations:

4. Rising domestic social preoccupations are likely to weaken or even fragment societal consensus.

5. An economic recession could threaten both Japanese democracy and Japanese-American ties, since both are still rather vulnerable.

6. A dramatic shift to the left is not likely during the next half-decade, though the left will grow in strength and become a more formidable facet of Japanese political life.

7. The LDP will try to co-opt the domestic programs of the left, but it itself will be less cohesive and may have to govern through coalitional arrangements.

8. Hence *sayonara* to certainty in Japanese political life; there will be, rather, more frequent realignments in the power leadership and even some political turmoil.

9. The overall mood of domestic politics is likely to involve a combination of rising rationalism and social radicalism.

10. Japan's economic situation is likely to become more complicated, particularly because of labor shortage, high ecological expenses, and a less favorable international context.

11. Some economic slowdown is to be expected, pushing Jap-

anese growth rates down to an average of about 8 percent per annum in the first half of this decade, and perhaps somewhat lower later.

12. It is doubtful that the vaunted style of Japanese decision-making, with its emphasis on consensus and collective responsibility, will work well under more critical circumstances.

13. Japan's foreign policy will strive to maximize options and reduce dependencies, with less reliance on the United States.

14.* Rising national ambitions will be frustrated by the absence of a coherent set of national goals, but the general trend will be toward a vague nationalist neutralism, without neutralist slogans or overt nationalism.

15. An Asian role for Japan is doubtful and undesirable.

16. Japanese policy toward Russia—in spite of increased Soviet cultivation—will be cool and calculating.

17. China will continue to have a special lure for Japan and will present, at least emotionally, an attractive option in the event of a dramatic rupture in relations with the United States, as well as be a source of acute political divisions within Japan.

18. 1975 will be a crucial year in Japanese-U.S. security relations and in Japan's security policy, with Japan inching up to a posture suited to the rapid implementation by that date of more basic security choices.

19. The nuclear option will be exercised if there is some basic deterioration in the international situation, with a more isolationist United States (especially if in the meantime humiliated somewhere by its adversaries) prompting the Japanese to assume their own strategic defense.

20. The worst possible combination for U.S.-Japanese relations is, therefore, an isolationist and protectionist United States,

* My original draft, written shortly after my return from Japan, had another item numbered 14 (with the total then being 23), which read as follows: "Tenacious rearguard action on the yen is to be expected, with the Japanese eventually yielding when confronted with the prospect of an international monetary crisis, but not before."

which would stimulate both Japanese militarism and nationalism.

21. Nonetheless, on the rational plane, both the Japanese and the Americans recognize the basic desirability of their alliance and will strive to maintain it through necessary accommodations.

22. The three fundamental problems in the Japanese-U.S. relation (economics, security, status) are not solvable within a bilateral framework.

The key contingency in the Japanese future is still the United States. American postwar policy toward Japan has been enlightened and, on the whole, successful. But the postwar period ended abruptly in August 1971, when President Nixon's initiatives toward China and in the monetary-economic field ushered in a new era in American-Japanese relations. Both sides must now make a very deliberate effort to safeguard what has been attained and to define new objectives. This is why it is now appropriate, although our report has focused on Japan and on the Japanese relationship to the United States, to make some recommendations concerning the American posture toward Japan.

The first is of a highly general character. America's understanding of and attention to Japanese matters is woefully inadequate. American reporting about Japan is disproportionately lower than American reporting of European matters; therefore, American newspapers, magazines, and television should pay consistently closer attention to Japanese developments. An average Japanese reads about the United States on the front page of his newspaper almost every day; an American reads about Japan only when something critical happens. Indeed, an American reads five times as much about West Germany as he reads about Japan.[1] Much the same goes for American studies of Japan, which lag behind Soviet studies, European studies, or Chinese studies. This breeds insensitivity and cultivates ignorance, which is simply incompatible with the fact that American-Japanese ties are *the* important ties in the Asian context.

Both on the mass and on the academic levels, major improvements are necessary, improvements that will require greater Japanese efforts. For many years the United States has stimulated and supported Japanese studies of America (through a large and expensive variety of programs). The Japanese have been delinquent in stimulating and supporting financially American studies of Japan. Some Japanese even feel, apparently, that it is better for foreigners not to understand Japan too well. Such an attitude is a mistake costly to good Japanese-American relations, and the Japanese—instead of criticizing U.S. inattentiveness to Japan—should make a very major effort to underwrite and stimulate in America broad programs of Japanese studies. Not to do so is to display the shortsightedness and the small-power mentality mentioned in our earlier discussions.

Connected to this point is the general problem of atmospherics and symbols. It is most unfortunate that President Nixon chose to announce his planned visit to Peking before going to Tokyo. The Japanese, given their sensitivity to international hierarchy, would have welcomed the American president eagerly, not only in order to erase the blemish associated with the abortion of Eisenhower's visit to Japan, but also to underline the preeminence of American-Japanese ties in the Pacific. It is therefore very important that the exchange of visits between the heads of state of Japan and the United States be undertaken with the most minute attention to detail and with every effort to assure their success.

The second recommendation concerns American attitudes toward Japan. It is both inaccurate and unwise to stimulate in the Japanese an exaggerated sense of their power in the world and to subject them to excessive and exaggerated flattery. Japan is a major force in the world, one of the truly great nations in the global mosaic, an unusually gifted and in many ways admirable people. Yet it is not a superpower and it is doubtful that it can become one. Indeed, efforts to become one—in part stimulated by excessive expectations that it will become one—

could become counterproductive, obscuring the sense of balance, the sense of restraint, as well as the sense of responsibility by which Japan should be guided as it assumes a major role in the world.

We should nurture, instead, Japanese realism. There is an ambivalent strand in the Japanese psyche: the hierarchical preoccupation and the competitive urge can easily get out of hand, even though in many practical matters the Japanese are extremely realistic. It is that realism which should be encouraged and offered real, as well as emotionally satisfying, outlets. It is, therefore, undesirable to speak of Japan as a superpower and to encourage a sense of inevitability (through the device of prediction that grows into desire) about Japan's acquisition of nuclear weaponry. Instead, it would be much better to seek to obtain for Japan a permanent seat on the Security Council of the United Nations, a position to which Japan has much more real claim than either France or Great Britain, and the assumption of which entails real and constructive international responsibilities. It should be a major objective of the United States to seek a revision of the United Nations Charter, seating Japan on the Security Council as one of the more important and influential states of the world.

The foregoing is related to the question of regional responsibility. I am doubtful, as I have already indicated, of the desirability of Japan assuming a special role in Asia, and especially dubious about the political benefit—either to Japan or to the United States—of the Japanization of Asian security. Since the Asians do not want it, the Japanese cannot do it. It would be much wiser for the United States to encourage broader Japanese involvement in international peace-keeping—for example, in the Middle East, where the Japanese have major interests—than for the United States to press the Japanese to become the protectors of Korea, Taiwan, and perhaps even Southeast Asia. A wider peace-keeping function, perhaps based formally on the device of individual "volunteers" coalescing outside of Japan into Japanese U.N. units (since the SDF is constitutionally forbidden from serving outside of Japan), would be an excellent way for Japan to assume a constructive and a more active global security role.

The problem of China, while a major issue in its own right, is related to the regional question. Boosting Japan as the main regional power in the Far East is tantamount to stimulating Japanese-Chinese rivalry. This may not be good for the stability of the region; efforts to that end will adversely affect American-Chinese relations and complicate both internal Japanese politics and Japanese-Chinese relations. Much to be preferred would be some effort to stimulate three-way Japanese-American-Chinese consultations on the economic-social problems of the region and eventually also on political-security matters. At first conducted through informal channels, such talks eventually could become more formal and develop into a standing conference.

The next two recommendations raise even more complicated issues, and they can only be treated here in broad outline form. The first of these—and this is the third recommendation—pertains to the nuclear issue. In my judgment, the United States should not encourage, at this time or in the very near future, Japan to go nuclear, because the decision to do so will inescapably generate profound fissures in the Japanese body politic, and even unpredictable international consequences. No self-evident benefit would thereby be secured by the United States. At the same time, active discouragement would be counterproductive, since it would simply irritate Japanese national feelings. A posture of noninvolvement, of "nuclear neutralism," is the wisest posture for the United States at this time, especially given the inclination of the Japanese to defer a clear-cut decision and to avoid the complications that the decision would generate.

However, it will become a different matter if and when Japan itself decides to go nuclear. That decision—if our analysis is sound—is likely to be taken in a setting that has itself become somewhat unfavorable to the United States. It is therefore important to bear in mind that it is not a forgone conclusion—indeed it is far from it—that Japan will actually go nuclear. But if it should, it actually may then be in the U.S. interest to assist the Japanese nuclear program, through direct technical assistance and perhaps also—as a transitional stage, prior to Japan's effective acquisition of nuclear weapons—through the so-called "two-key" system with regard to nuclear weapons targeted on Japan's potential enemies. For one thing, the United States will then need allies even more than before, and hence it will not be in a favorable position actively to oppose the Japanese decision. Secondly, and more problematically, it can be argued that, in a setting of U.S. nuclear superiority, nuclear proliferation is definitely contrary to U.S. interests; in a setting of parity (not to speak of U.S. nuclear disadvantage), proliferation may be advantageous to the United States in that it will complicate the strategic and political planning particularly of the power that then enjoys the nuclear edge.

To be sure, advocacy of U.S. assistance to the Japanese nuclear defense program can be tantamount to encouraging Japan to go nuclear, something I have warned against. This inconsistency is more apparent than real. My argument is that, other things remaining constant, Japan is not likely to go nuclear; it is likely to go nuclear in the event of a major shift in world affairs—and, at that point, positive U.S. aid to Japan will be preferable to the other alternatives outlined in our earlier discussion. Short of such a basic change, the Japanese realization that the decision to go nuclear would precipitate major international complications for Japan, including adverse consequences in the Japanese-American relationship, is a strong deterrent, reinforcing the other domestic obstacles to such a decision.

In the meantime, the United States would be well advised to upgrade American-Japanese strategic-political planning and to reduce the more visible manifestations of its military presence in Japan, concentrating more on joint basing and on the maintenance in a state of high readiness of facilities for emergency deployment. A more direct Japanese financial contribution for the maintenance of the United States strategic deterrent, and wider Japanese participation in the process of strategic planning, also seem appropriate, perhaps through the mechanism of joint high-level civilian-military planning staffs. The purpose of such staffs would be to develop wider reciprocal understanding of the likely circumstances under which it would be in the Japanese and American interest to act jointly. However, there is an undeniable circularity involved in the argument here: a continued U.S. military presence in Japan offends Japanese nationalism and creates strains in the U.S.-Japanese relationship; a reduced U.S. presence in Japan, which intensifies Japanese insecurity, increases the need for larger Japanese armed forces and gives rise elsewhere to renewed fears of Japanese militarism. Under the circumstances, the most that can be done is for both the Japanese and the Americans to try to harmonize gradual change in their military relationship with a gradually surfacing sense of Japanese national self-assertiveness.

Insofar as Japanese security is concerned, the United States would also be wise to back and perhaps even very quietly support the emergence of a Pacific maritime triangle, based on the insular constellations of Japan, Indonesia, and Australia. The three together have certain overlapping security problems and meshing economic interests. The Pacific maritime triangle—though not necessarily a formal alliance, and with the United States indirectly associated with it—could be a source of stability and wider cooperation, without precipitating fears of Japanese domination.

This brings us to our last point. It is unlikely that the problems of security, or that of status or that of economics in the Japanese-American relationship can any longer be adequately handled on a purely bilateral basis. The question of security will require in the years ahead, above all, far greater meshing of minds on political-strategic trends in the region as a whole, and even worldwide. This means a continuing process of consultation concerning the likely threats, the possible contingencies, and common objectives. Such a process cannot involve the United States and Japan alone, but must include also other interested powers, such as Australia, Korea, perhaps Indonesia, and so forth. Under certain circumstances, it could also involve NATO. What is needed, therefore, is not a new alliance, but some machinery that insures such consultations among interested parties, not necessarily on the basis of binding obligations, but out of common interests.

The need to transform the American-Japanese relationship into something wider and more globally constructive is even more evident with regard to the problems of economics and status. This does not mean that bilateral efforts to resolve economic difficulties are futile—quite the contrary. Much more needs to be done both on the American and on the Japanese side to anticipate bilateral difficulties in the very large trade between the two countries. As in the political-military field, so in economics a standing joint consultative machinery—and not only ad hoc-level meetings—is very much needed, in order to anticipate likely difficulties and to develop over time mutually acceptable regulatory procedures. Both sides should have learned by now that ad hoc resolution of problems usually means dealing with the problems when they become painfully acute.

Moreover, the Japanese must learn that foreign investment in their country can be mutually beneficial and that it does not lead to foreign domination. Western Europe has benefited technologically and economically from American investment, without loss of political independence. France is a good example. Moreover, the Japanese can hardly expect to step up their own foreign investment abroad without opening themselves to foreign investment. Their continuing restrictions on foreign investments are, in the final analysis, an expression of an insular orientation that is incompatible with Japan's growing international involvement.

Beyond that, the American-Japanese economic relationship has to be set in a wider framework. The emergence of the Common Market highlights the fact that, increasingly, the three economic pillars of possible global stability and cooperation are the United States, Japan, and Western Europe. Staged movement toward a free trade area among these larger units, as well as among some of the other advanced economies closely associated with the three, would make it easier to reduce the strains and imbalances that prevail in a more limited bilateral relationship. An international division of labor, which some leading economists have been urging, could then more easily emerge, permitting broader and more indirect exchanges of goods, services, and products, reducing bilateral strains and imbalances. A number of Japanese have signaled their interest in such a wider arrangement,[2] and its benefits would spill over into the political realm as well, particularly in regard to the elusive question of status.

In a bilateral U.S.-Japanese relationship, Japan will remain the weaker and hence a somewhat uneasy partner. Such a condition inevitably breeds continuing resentments, while occasional acts of American insensitivity produce injured pride and gnawing suspicions. A wide cooperative framework, involving a gradual process of shaping a community of the developed nations, would put Japan in the front rank of a global effort to provide for more orderly and satisfactory international political and economic relations. Such a community of the developed nations would not be just a rich man's club; indeed, one of its key purposes would be to undertake a more rational and cooperative effort to help the less developed countries. It would not—or should not—be meant to be a new anti-Communist alliance; indeed, by reducing the temptations in Moscow or Peking to play on national rivalries and by deliberately inviting Communist states into those areas of cooperation for which they are suited, either by the level of their development or by their particular location, the community of the developed nations would help to terminate gradually the ideological global civil war. For the American-Japanese relationship, a wider framework would have the added advantage of simultaneously encouraging the internationalization of Japan without that internationalization being tantamount to Americanization. The latter is understandably resented; the former is needed.

A community of the developed nations is gradually emerging anyway, but more deliberate steps are needed to give this process direction and purpose, and to offset the tensions affecting the Japanese-American relationship. To that end, regular annual meetings of heads of state of Japan, western Europe, and the United States are desirable, as well as some stand-by consultative-planning machinery. Over time, this would help to stimulate common perspectives and programs. Three-way consultations between parliamentarians should similarly be institutionalized. Alongside the above, more informal three-way contacts are needed; a continuous dialogue among the social elites of the three entities needs to be stimulated, just as the Monnet Action Committee and the Bilderberg Meeting contributed so much to the emergence of the European identity and to an Atlantic spirit of cooperation. More active Japanese participation—personal and financial—in international corporations would also be a constructive part of this process.

Seen in a broader historical perspective, America, western Europe and Japan are sharing in common a unique experience: they are in the vanguard of societies leaving the industrial age and beginning to confront the challenge of the new technetronic era.[3] They thus confront similar problems with their younger people, as well as a broader transformation of values; they share some of the same social dilemmas; because of their wealth, they also shoulder similar responsibilities in regard to the less fortunate portions of mankind. Moreover, Japan, western Europe, and America are linked by still one further very important similarity: they operate within a framework of democratic institutions that, though far from perfect, represent the most decent and just system of government so far devised by man. Taken together, the above do provide a point of departure for common and more constructive efforts.

The key point to bear in mind is that Japan is now entering the world on a massive scale. The process may either be disruptive of existing Japanese external relations and of its domestic stability, or it can become a vital link in a wider pattern of global cooperation. Neither outcome is inevitable—and both the Japanese and the Americans have a vital stake in which it will be.

Source Notes

INTRODUCTION

1. To name but a few: Edwin Reischauer, Henry Rosovsky, Herbert Passin, Gerald Curtis, James Morley, Robert Scalapino, Robert Ward, and others.
2. Yasunari Kawabata, *Japan the Beautiful and Myself* (Tokyo: The Nobel Foundation, 1968), p. 56.

1. SOCIAL PATTERNS

1. *Asahi Evening News,* May 15, 1971.
2. *The Japan Times,* May 22, 1971.
3. For specific details of the financial expenditures envisaged, see ibid., May 26, 1971.
4. Herbert Passin, "The Future," in Herbert Passin, ed., *The United States and Japan* (Englewood Cliffs, N.J.: Prentice-Hall, Inc., 1966), p. 146.
5. See on this point Kishimoto Hideo, "Some Japanese Cultural Traits and Religions," in Charles A. Moore, ed., *The Japanese Mind* (Honolulu: East-West Center Press, 1967), p. 118.

6. Y. Hideki, "Modern Trends of Western Civilization and Cultural Peculiarities in Japan," in Moore, *The Japanese Mind,* p. 58.

3. ECONOMIC PROSPECTS

1. Henry Rosovsky, "A Memorandum from the Devil's Advocate," mimeographed, Harvard University (1970), p. 36.
2. *Economic Picture of Japan* (Tokyo: Keidanren, 1971), p. 24.
3. General Council of Trade Unions of Japan [SOHYO], "White Paper on Wages for 1971," Tokyo, January 15, 1971, p. 63. This document is a very valuable source on the social conditions of Japanese labor.
4. *Harvard Business Review,* March–April 1971.
5. Chie Nakane, *Japanese Society* (London: Weidenfeld and Nicolson, 1970), p. 145.
6. Ibid., p. 35.
7. For a comprehensive and able report, see *Computer White Paper* (Tokyo: Japan Computer Usage Development Institute), 1970.

4. IN SEARCH OF A ROLE

1. Nobuhiko Ushiba, "Some Thoughts on the 1970s" (Tokyo: Public Information Bureau of the Ministry of Foreign Affairs, 1969), p. 9.
2. Fuji Kamiya, "Japan's International Environment in the 1970s," *Chuo Koron,* October 1969, p. 110.
3. "Charting the Course of Japan in the '70s" (Tokyo: Keizai Doyukai [Japan Committee for Economic Development], April 1970), p. 9.
4. Edwin Reischauer, *The United States and Japan,* 3rd ed. (Cambridge, Mass.: Harvard University Press, 1965), p. 110.
5. Kinhite Mushakoji, "The View From Japan," in Herbert Passin, ed., *The United States and Japan* (Englewood Cliffs, N.J.: Prentice-Hall Inc., 1966), p. 131.
6. I hope that I have not done injustice to the extremely suggestive points made to me by Professor Hideo Itokawa. On the general relationship between Japanese language and Japanese mode of thinking, I found the views of Kishimoto Hideo ("Some Japanese Cultural Traits and Religions," in Charles A. Moore, ed., *The Japanese Mind* [Honolulu: East-West Center Press, 1967], especially pp. 110–112) very perceptive and confirmed by my experiences while in Japan.
7. For example, a good case to this effect is made by Kei

Waikuzumi, "Japan Beyond 1970," *Foreign Affairs,* April 1969, pp. 514–515.

8. Good background material is contained in a study by Saburo Okita, *Essays in Japan and Asia,* (Tokyo: Japan Economic Research Center, 1970).
9. See Okita, *Essays in Japan and Asia,* p. 72.
10. Some of Japan's top businessmen have recently voiced skepticism concerning such a Japanese role in Asia. See, for example, the *Keidanren Review,* no. 17 (Winter 1971), in which several of Japan's top businessmen express strong skepticism concerning that notion. For a more generalized and very thoughtful critique, see Kinhite Mushakoji, "Towards a Japanese Foreign Policy," *Chuo Koron,* July 1970, where the idea of Japanese leadership in Asia is explicitly criticized.
11. Mayasa Miyoshi, "Japan's International Trade and Investment Policies for the 1970s" [paper read to a joint Keidanren–Atlantic Institute Conference, Tokyo, March 1971], p. 22.
12. For a good overall discussion, particularly of the decision-making process, see David I. Hitchcock, Jr., "Joint Development of Siberia: Decision-Making in Japanese-Soviet Relations," *Asian Survey,* March 1971.

5. SECURITY AND STATUS

1. Speaking before the Foreign Correspondents Club in Japan, March 5, 1970.
2. Kei Wakaizumi, "Japan Beyond 1970," *Foreign Affairs,* April 1969, pp. 513–514.
3. *Mainichi Shimbun,* April 28, 1971. The same story contains a great deal of detail concerning growing competition among Japanese industrial firms for defense orders for a great variety of armaments, including some highly sophisticated items.
4. A discussion of these restrictions as well as some data on the rapidly expanding Japanese arms exports are contained in *Asahi Shimbun,* February 16, 1971.
5. *Mainichi Shimbun,* April 23, 1971.
6. This paraphrases the recommendation of Kiichi Saeki, "Security Problems in the '70s," *Ushio,* January–February 1970.
7. Genko Uchida, "Principles of Foreign Policy in the Age of Technology," *Chuo Koron,* March 1970.
8. One Japanese strategic thinker has come close to suggesting such a possibility. See Makoto Momoi, "Australia and Japan," in H. G. Gelber, ed., *Problems of Australian Defense* (Melbourne–London: Oxford University Press, 1970).

6. THE RELATIONSHIP WITH THE UNITED STATES

1. For a good example of this viewpoint, see *Asahi Shimbun,* May 20, 1956.
2. "Generally speaking, America has become tired" (Masasaka Kosaka, "Thinking About Japan-U.S. Relations in the 1970s," *Bungei Shunju,* September 1970). For a broader but very influential indictment of American social developments, see Yonosuke Nagai, "Disintegrating America—Ecology of Crisis," *Chuo Koron,* September 1970.
3. Chikara Makino, "Japan-United States Relations," *Tsusan Journal* 3–4 (1970). Makino's paper is an extremely thoughtful and perceptive analysis of the American-Japanese relationship, involving many personal insights, his official position notwithstanding.
4. John Toland, *The Rising Sun* (New York: 1970), p. 106.
5. Kosaka, "Thinking About Japan-U.S. Relations."
6. Ibid.
7. Makino, "Japan-United States Relations."

CONCLUSIONS AND RECOMMENDATIONS

1. L. H. Gelb, "U.S. Domestic Politics and U.S.-Japan Relations" (paper presented to the meeting on "The United States and Japan in Asia," sponsored by the Japan Institute on International Affairs and the Brookings Institution, March 1971), pp. 14–15.
2. See particularly Nobuyoshi Namiki, "Japan's International Course in the '70s," *Chuo Koron,* January 1970. Mr. Namiki is a higher official in MITI. See also Yoshihane Iwasa, "Japan-U.S. Economic Cooperation with Asia in the '70s," *Pacific Community,* April 1970, which urges something similar, although somewhat more cautiously.
3. For a fuller account, see my *Between Two Ages: America's Role in the Technetronic Era* (New York: Viking Press, 1970), especially pp. 293–311.

Index

About the Author

Zbigniew Brzezinski received his B.A. from McGill University and his Ph.D. from Harvard University. He is Director of the Research Institute of Communist Affairs and Herbert Lehman Professor of Government at Columbia University. His most recent book is *Between Two Ages*.

72 73 74 75 10 9 8 7 6 5 4 3 2 1

Revised January, 1970

harper torchbooks

<u>*American Studies: General*</u>

HENRY STEELE COMMAGER, Ed.: The Struggle for Racial Equality TB/1300

CARL N. DEGLER: Out of Our Past: *The Forces that Shaped Modern America* CN/2

CARL N. DEGLER, Ed.: Pivotal Interpretations of American History Vol. I TB/1240; Vol. II TB/1241

A. S. EISENSTADT, Ed.: The Craft of American History: *Selected Essays* Vol. I TB/1255; Vol. II TB/1256

ROBERT L. HEILBRONER: The Limits of American Capitalism TB/1305

JOHN HIGHAM, Ed.: The Reconstruction of American History TB/1068

ROBERT H. JACKSON: The Supreme Court in the American System of Government TB/1106

JOHN F. KENNEDY: A Nation of Immigrants. *Illus. Revised and Enlarged. Introduction by Robert F. Kennedy* TB/1118

RICHARD B. MORRIS: Fair Trial: *Fourteen Who Stood Accused, from Anne Hutchinson to Alger Hiss* TB/1335

GUNNAR MYRDAL: An American Dilemma: *The Negro Problem and Modern Democracy. Introduction by the Author.* Vol. I TB/1443; Vol. II TB/1444

GILBERT OSOFSKY, Ed.: The Burden of Race: *A Documentary History of Negro-White Relations in America* TB/1405

ARNOLD ROSE: The Negro in America: *The Condensed Version of Gunnar Myrdal's* An American Dilemma. *Second Edition* TB/3048

JOHN E. SMITH: Themes in American Philosophy: *Purpose, Experience and Community* TB/1466

WILLIAM R. TAYLOR: Cavalier and Yankee: *The Old South and American National Character* TB/1474

<u>*American Studies: Colonial*</u>

BERNARD BAILYN: The New England Merchants in the Seventeenth Century TB/1149

ROBERT E. BROWN: Middle-Class Democracy and Revolution in Massachusetts, 1691–1780. *New Introduction by Author* TB/1413

JOSEPH CHARLES: The Origins of the American Party System TB/1049

WESLEY FRANK CRAVEN: The Colonies in Transition: 1660-1712† TB/3084

CHARLES GIBSON: Spain in America † TB/3077

CHARLES GIBSON, Ed.: The Spanish Tradition in America + HR/1351

LAWRENCE HENRY GIPSON: The Coming of the Revolution: 1763-1775. † *Illus.* TB/3007

PERRY MILLER: Errand Into the Wilderness TB/1139

PERRY MILLER & T. H. JOHNSON, Eds.: The Puritans: *A Sourcebook of Their Writings* Vol. I TB/1093; Vol. II TB/1094

EDMUND S. MORGAN: The Puritan Family: *Religion and Domestic Relations in Seventeenth Century New England* TB/1227

WALLACE NOTESTEIN: The English People on the Eve of Colonization: 1603-1630. † *Illus.* TB/3006

LOUIS B. WRIGHT: The Cultural Life of the American Colonies: 1607-1763. † *Illus.* TB/3005

<u>*American Studies: The Revolution to 1860*</u>

JOHN R. ALDEN: The American Revolution: 1775-1783. † *Illus.* TB/3011

RAY A. BILLINGTON: The Far Western Frontier: 1830-1860. † *Illus.* TB/3012

GEORGE DANGERFIELD: The Awakening of American Nationalism, 1815-1828. † *Illus.* TB/3061

CLEMENT EATON: The Growth of Southern Civilization, 1790-1860. † *Illus.* TB/3040

LOUIS FILLER: The Crusade against Slavery: 1830-1860. † *Illus.* TB/3029

WILLIM W. FREEHLING: Prelude to Civil War: *The Nullification Controversy in South Carolina, 1816-1836* TB/1359

THOMAS JEFFERSON: Notes on the State of Virginia. ‡ *Edited by Thomas P. Abernethy* TB/3052

JOHN C. MILLER: The Federalist Era: 1789-1801. † *Illus.* TB/3027

RICHARD B. MORRIS: The American Revolution Reconsidered TB/1363

GILBERT OSOFSKY, Ed.: Puttin' On Ole Massa: *The Slave Narratives of Henry Bibb, William Wells Brown, and Solomon Northup* ‡ TB/1432

FRANCIS S. PHILBRICK: The Rise of the West, 1754-1830. † *Illus.* TB/3067

MARSHALL SMELSER: The Democratic Republic, 1801-1815 † TB/1406

† The New American Nation Series, edited by Henry Steele Commager and Richard B. Morris.
‡ American Perspectives series, edited by Bernard Wishy and William E. Leuchtenburg.
a History of Europe series, edited by J. H. Plumb.
§ The Library of Religion and Culture, edited by Benjamin Nelson.
‖ Researches in the Social, Cultural, and Behavioral Sciences, edited by Benjamin Nelson.
Σ Harper Modern Science Series, edited by James A. Newman.
° Not for sale in Canada.
+ Documentary History of the United States series, edited by Richard B. Morris.
# Documentary History of Western Civilization series, edited by Eugene C. Black and Leonard W. Levy.
^ The Economic History of the United States series, edited by Henry David et al.
¶ European Perspectives series, edited by Eugene C. Black.
** Contemporary Essays series, edited by Leonard W. Levy.
* The Stratum Series, edited by John Hale.

LOUIS B. WRIGHT: Culture on the Moving Frontier TB/1053

American Studies: The Civil War to 1900

T. C. COCHRAN & WILLIAM MILLER: The Age of Enterprise: *A Social History of Industrial America* TB/1054

W. A. DUNNING: Reconstruction, Political and Economic: 1865-1877 TB/1073

HAROLD U. FAULKNER: Politics, Reform and Expansion: 1890-1900. † *Illus.* TB/3020

GEORGE M. FREDRICKSON: The Inner Civil War: *Northern Intellectuals and the Crisis of the Union* TB/1358

JOHN A. GARRATY: The New Commonwealth, 1877-1890 † TB/1410

HELEN HUNT JACKSON: A Century of Dishonor: *The Early Crusade for Indian Reform. † Edited by Andrew F. Rolle* TB/3063

WILLIAM G. MCLOUGHLIN, Ed.: The American Evangelicals, 1800-1900: An Anthology ‡ TB/1382

JAMES S. PIKE: The Prostrate State: *South Carolina under Negro Government. ‡ Intro. by Robert F. Durden* TB/3085

VERNON LANE WHARTON: The Negro in Mississippi, 1865-1890 TB/1178

American Studies: The Twentieth Century

RAY STANNARD BAKER: Following the Color Line: *American Negro Citizenship in Progressive Era. ‡ Edited by Dewey W. Grantham, Jr. Illus.* TB/3053

RANDOLPH S. BOURNE: War and the Intellectuals: *Collected Essays, 1915-1919. ‡ Edited by Carl Resek* TB/3043

A. RUSSELL BUCHANAN: The United States and World War II. † *Illus.* Vol. I TB/3044; Vol. II TB/3045

THOMAS C. COCHRAN: The American Business System: *A Historical Perspective, 1900-1955* TB/1080

FOSTER RHEA DULLES: America's Rise to World Power: 1898-1954. † *Illus.* TB/3021

HAROLD U. FAULKNER: The Decline of Laissez Faire, 1897-1917 TB/1397

JOHN D. HICKS: Republican Ascendancy: 1921-1933. † *Illus.* TB/3041

WILLIAM E. LEUCHTENBURG: Franklin D. Roosevelt and the New Deal: 1932-1940. † *Illus.* TB/3025

WILLIAM E. LEUCHTENBURG, Ed.: The New Deal: *A Documentary History* + HR/1354

ARTHUR S. LINK: Woodrow Wilson and the Progressive Era: 1910-1917. † *Illus.* TB/3023

BROADUS MITCHELL: Depression Decade: *From New Era through New Deal, 1929-1941* ^ TB/1439

GEORGE E. MOWRY: The Era of Theodore Roosevelt and the Birth of Modern America: 1900-1912. † *Illus.* TB/3022

WILLIAM PRESTON, JR.: Aliens and Dissenters:

TWELVE SOUTHERNERS: I'll Take My Stand: *The South and the Agrarian Tradition. Intro. by Louis D. Rubin, Jr.; Biographical Essays by Virginia Rock* TB/1072

Art, Art History, Aesthetics

ERWIN PANOFSKY: Renaissance and Renascences in Western Art. *Illus.* TB/1447

ERWIN PANOFSKY: Studies in Iconology: *Humanistic Themes in the Art of the Renaissance. 180 illus.* TB/1077

HEINRICH ZIMMER: Myths and Symbols in Indian Art and Civilization. *70 illus.* TB/2005

Asian Studies

WOLFGANG FRANKE: China and the West: *The Cultural Encounter, 13th to 20th Centuries. Trans. by R. A. Wilson* TB/1326

L. CARRINGTON GOODRICH: A Short History of the Chinese People. *Illus.* TB/3015

Economics & Economic History

C. E. BLACK: The Dynamics of Modernization: *A Study in Comparative History* TB/1321

GILBERT BURCK & EDITORS OF *Fortune:* The Computer Age: *And its Potential for Management* TB/1179

ROBERT L. HEILBRONER: The Future as History: *The Historic Currents of Our Time and the Direction in Which They Are Taking America* TB/1386

ROBERT L. HEILBRONER: The Great Ascent: *The Struggle for Economic Development in Our Time* TB/3030

FRANK H. KNIGHT: The Economic Organization TB/1214

DAVID S. LANDES: Bankers and Pashas: *International Finance and Economic Imperialism in Egypt. New Preface by the Author* TB/1412

ROBERT LATOUCHE: The Birth of Western Economy: *Economic Aspects of the Dark Ages* TB/1290

W. ARTHUR LEWIS: The Principles of Economic Planning. *New Introduction by the Author°* TB/1436

WILLIAM MILLER, Ed.: Men in Business: *Essays on the Historical Role of the Entrepreneur* TB/1081

HERBERT A. SIMON: The Shape of Automation: *For Men and Management* TB/1245

Historiography and History of Ideas

J. BRONOWSKI & BRUCE MAZLISH: The Western Intellectual Tradition: *From Leonardo to Hegel* TB/3001

WILHELM DILTHEY: Pattern and Meaning in History: *Thoughts on History and Society.° Edited with an Intro. by H. P. Rickman* TB/1075

J. H. HEXTER: More's Utopia: *The Biography of an Idea. Epilogue by the Author* TB/1195

H. STUART HUGHES: History as Art and as Science: *Twin Vistas on the Past* TB/1207

ARTHUR O. LOVEJOY: The Great Chain of Being: *A Study of the History of an Idea* TB/1009

RICHARD H. POPKIN: The History of Scepticism from Erasmus to Descartes. *Revised Edition* TB/1391

BRUNO SNELL: The Discovery of the Mind: *The Greek Origins of European Thought* TB/1018

History: General

HANS KOHN: The Age of Nationalism: *The First Era of Global History* TB/1380

BERNARD LEWIS: The Arabs in History TB/1029

BERNARD LEWIS: The Middle East and the West ° TB/1274

History: Ancient

A. ANDREWS: The Greek Tyrants TB/1103

THEODOR H. GASTER: Thespis: *Ritual Myth and Drama in the Ancient Near East* TB/1281

A. H. M. JONES, Ed.: A History of Rome through the Fifth Century # *Vol. I: The Republic* HR/1364
Vol. II The Empire: HR/1460

SAMUEL NOAH KRAMER: Sumerian Mythology TB/1055

NAPHTALI LEWIS & MEYER REINHOLD, Eds.: Roman Civilization *Vol. I: The Republic* TB/1231
Vol. II: The Empire TB/1232

History: Medieval

NORMAN COHN: The Pursuit of the Millennium: *Revolutionary Messianism in Medieval and Reformation Europe* TB/1037

F. L. GANSHOF: Feudalism TB/1058

F. L. GANSHOF: The Middle Ages: *A History of International Relations. Translated by Rêmy Hall* TB/1411

HENRY CHARLES LEA: The Inquisition of the Middle Ages. || *Introduction by Walter Ullmann* TB/1456

History: Renaissance & Reformation

JACOB BURCKHARDT: The Civilization of the Renaissance in Italy. *Introduction by Benjamin Nelson and Charles Trinkaus. Illus.* Vol. I TB/40; Vol. II TB/41

JOHN CALVIN & JACOPO SADOLETO: A Reformation Debate. *Edited by John C. Olin* TB/1239

J. H. ELLIOTT: Europe Divided, 1559-1598 *a* ° TB/1414

G. R. ELTON: Reformation Europe, 1517-1559 ° *a* TB/1270

HANS J. HILLERBRAND, Ed., The Protestant Reformation # HR/1342

JOHAN HUIZINGA: Erasmus and the Age of Reformation. *Illus.* TB/19

JOEL HURSTFIELD: The Elizabethan Nation TB/1312

JOEL HURSTFIELD, Ed.: The Reformation Crisis TB/1267

PAUL OSKAR KRISTELLER: Renaissance Thought: *The Classic, Scholastic, and Humanist Strains* TB/1048

DAVID LITTLE: Religion, Order and Law: *A Study in Pre-Revolutionary England. § Preface by R. Bellah* TB/1418

PAOLO ROSSI: Philosophy, Technology, and the Arts, in the Early Modern Era 1400-1700. || *Edited by Benjamin Nelson. Translated by Salvator Attanasio* TB/1458

H. R. TREVOR-ROPER: The European Witch-craze of the Sixteenth and Seventeenth Centuries and Other Essays ° TB/1416

History: Modern European

ALAN BULLOCK: Hitler, A Study in Tyranny. ° *Revised Edition. Illus.* TB/1123

JOHANN GOTTLIEB FICHTE: Addresses to the German Nation. *Ed. with Intro. by George A. Kelly* ¶ TB/1366

ALBERT GOODWIN: The French Revolution TB/1064

STANLEY HOFFMANN et al.: In Search of France: *The Economy, Society and Political System In the Twentieth Century* TB/1219

H. STUART HUGHES: The Obstructed Path: *French Social Thought in the Years of Desperation* TB/1451

JOHAN HUIZINGA: Dutch Civilisation in the 17th Century and Other Essays TB/1453

JOHN MCMANNERS: European History, 1789-1914: *Men, Machines and Freedom* TB/1419

HUGH SETON-WATSON: Eastern Europe Between the Wars, 1918-1941 TB/1330

ALBERT SOREL: Europe Under the Old Regime. *Translated by Francis H. Herrick* TB/1121

A. J. P. TAYLOR: From Napoleon to Lenin: *Historical Essays* ° TB/1268

A. J. P. TAYLOR: The Habsburg Monarchy, 1809-1918: *A History of the Austrian Empire and Austria-Hungary* ° TB/1187

J. M. THOMPSON: European History, 1494-1789 TB/1431

H. R. TREVOR-ROPER: Historical Essays TB/1269

Literature & Literary Criticism

W. J. BATE: From Classic to Romantic: *Premises of Taste in Eighteenth Century England* TB/1036

VAN WYCK BROOKS: Van Wyck Brooks: The Early Years: *A Selection from his Works, 1908-1921 Ed. with Intro. by Claire Sprague* TB/3082

RICHMOND LATTIMORE, Translator: The Odyssey of Homer TB/1389

ROBERT PREYER, Ed.: Victorian Literature ** TB/1302

Philosophy

HENRI BERGSON: Time and Free Will: *An Essay on the Immediate Data of Consciousness* ° TB/1021

H. J. BLACKHAM: Six Existentialist Thinkers: *Kierkegaard, Nietzsche, Jaspers, Marcel, Heidegger, Sartre* ° TB/1002

J. M. BOCHENSKI: The Methods of Contemporary Thought. *Trans. by Peter Caws* TB/1377

ERNST CASSIRER: Rousseau, Kant and Goethe. *Intro. by Peter Gay* TB/1092

MICHAEL GELVEN: A Commentary on Heidegger's "Being and Time" TB/1464

J. GLENN GRAY: Hegel and Greek Thought TB/1409

W. K. C. GUTHRIE: The Greek Philosophers: *From Thales to Aristotle* ° TB/1008

G. W. F. HEGEL: Phenomenology of Mind. ° || *Introduction by George Lichtheim* TB/1303

MARTIN HEIDEGGER: Discourse on Thinking. *Translated with a Preface by John M. Anderson and E. Hans Freund. Introduction by John M. Anderson* TB/1459

F. H. HEINEMANN: Existentialism and the Modern Predicament TB/28

WERER HEISENBERG: Physics and Philosophy: *The Revolution in Modern Science. Intro. by F. S. C. Northrop* TB/549

EDMUND HUSSERL: Phenomenology and the Crisis of Philosophy. § *Translated with an Introduction by Quentin Lauer* TB/1170

IMMANUEL KANT: Groundwork of the Metaphysic of Morals. *Translated and Analyzed by H. J. Paton* TB/1159

WALTER KAUFMANN, Ed.: Religion From Tolstoy to Camus: *Basic Writings on Religious Truth and Morals* TB/123

QUENTIN LAUER: Phenomenology: *Its Genesis and Prospect. Preface by Aron Gurwitsch* TB/1169

MICHAEL POLANYI: Personal Knowledge: *Towards a Post-Critical Philosophy* TB/1158

WILLARD VAN ORMAN QUINE: Elementary Logic *Revised Edition* TB/577

WILHELM WINDELBAND: A History of Philosophy *Vol. I: Greek, Roman, Medieval* TB/38

Vol. II: Renaissance, Enlightenment, Modern TB/39
LUDWIG WITTGENSTEIN: The Blue and Brown Books ° TB/1211
LUDWIG WITTGENSTEIN: Notebooks, 1914-1916 TB/1441

Political Science & Government

C. E. BLACK: The Dynamics of Modernization: *A Study in Comparative History* TB/1321
DENIS W. BROGAN: Politics in America. *New Introduction by the Author* TB/1469
ROBERT CONQUEST: Power and Policy in the USSR: *The Study of Soviet Dynastics* ° TB/1307
JOHN B. MORRALL: Political Thought in Medieval Times TB/1076
KARL R. POPPER: The Open Society and Its Enemies *Vol. I: The Spell of Plato* TB/1101
Vol. II: The High Tide of Prophecy: Hegel, Marx, and the Aftermath TB/1102
HENRI DE SAINT-SIMON: Social Organization, The Science of Man, and Other Writings. || *Edited and Translated with an Introduction by Felix Markham* TB/1152
CHARLES SCHOTTLAND, Ed.: The Welfare State ** TB/1323
JOSEPH A. SCHUMPETER: Capitalism, Socialism and Democracy TB/3008

Psychology

LUDWIG BINSWANGER: Being-in-the-World: *Selected Papers. || Trans. with Intro. by Jacob Needleman* TB/1365
MIRCEA ELIADE: Cosmos and History: *The Myth of the Eternal Return* § TB/2050
MIRCEA ELIADE: Myth and Reality TB/1369
SIGMUND FREUD: On Creativity and the Unconscious: *Papers on the Psychology of Art, Literature, Love, Religion. § Intro. by Benjamin Nelson* TB/45
J. GLENN GRAY: The Warriors: *Reflections on Men in Battle. Introduction by Hannah Arendt* TB/1294
WILLIAM JAMES: Psychology: *The Briefer Course. Edited with an Intro. by Gordon Allport* TB/1034

Religion: Ancient and Classical, Biblical and Judaic Traditions

MARTIN BUBER: Eclipse of God: *Studies in the Relation Between Religion and Philosophy* TB/12
MARTIN BUBER: Hasidism and Modern Man. *Edited and Translated by Maurice Friedman* TB/839
MARTIN BUBER: The Knowledge of Man. *Edited with an Introduction by Maurice Friedman. Translated by Maurice Friedman and Ronald Gregor Smith* TB/135
MARTIN BUBER: Moses. *The Revelation and the Covenant* TB/837
MARTIN BUBER: The Origin and Meaning of Hasidism. *Edited and Translated by Maurice Friedman* TB/835
MARTIN BUBER: The Prophetic Faith TB/73
MARTIN BUBER: Two Types of Faith: *Interpenetration of Judaism and Christianity* ° TB/75
M. S. ENSLIN: Christian Beginnings TB/5
M. S. ENSLIN: The Literature of the Christian Movement TB/6
HENRI FRANKFORT: Ancient Egyptian Religion: *An Interpretation* TB/77

Religion: Early Christianity Through Reformation

ANSELM OF CANTERBURY: Truth, Freedom, and Evil: *Three Philosophical Dialogues. Edited and Translated by Jasper Hopkins and Herbert Richardson* TB/317
EDGAR J. GOODSPEED: A Life of Jesus TB/1
ROBERT M. GRANT: Gnosticism and Early Christianity TB/136

Religion: Oriental Religions

TOR ANDRAE: Mohammed: *The Man and His Faith* § TB/62
EDWARD CONZE: Buddhism: *Its Essence and Development. ° Foreword by Arthur Waley* TB/58
H. G. CREEL: Confucius and the Chinese Way TB/63
FRANKLIN EDGERTON, Trans. & Ed.: The Bhagavad Gita TB/115
SWAMI NIKHILANANDA, Trans. & Ed.: The Upanishads TB/114
D. T. SUZUKI: On Indian Mahayana Buddhism. ° *Ed. with Intro. by Edward Conze.* TB/1403

Science and Mathematics

W. E. LE GROS CLARK: The Antecedents of Man: *An Introduction to the Evolution of the Primates. ° Illus.* TB/559
ROBERT E. COKER: Streams, Lakes, Ponds. *Illus.* TB/586
ROBERT E. COKER: This Great and Wide Sea: *An Introduction to Oceanography and Marine Biology. Illus.* TB/551
WILLARD VAN ORMAN QUINE: Mathematical Logic TB/558

Sociology and Anthropology

REINHARD BENDIX: Work and Authority in Industry: *Ideologies of Management in the Course of Industrialization* TB/3035
KENNETH B. CLARK: Dark Ghetto: *Dilemmas of Social Power. Foreword by Gunnar Myrdal* TB/1317
KENNETH CLARK & JEANNETTE HOPKINS: A Relevant War Against Poverty: *A Study of Community Action Programs and Observable Social Change* TB/1480
LEWIS COSER, Ed.: Political Sociology TB/1293
GARY T. MARX: Protest and Prejudice: *A Study of Belief in the Black Community* TB/1435
ROBERT K. MERTON, LEONARD BROOM, LEONARD S. COTTRELL, JR., Editors: Sociology Today: *Problems and Prospects* || Vol. I TB/1173; Vol. II TB/1174
GILBERT OSOFSKY, Ed.: The Burden of Race: A Documentary History of Negro-White Relations in America TB/1405
GILBERT OSOFSKY: Harlem: The Making of a Ghetto: *Negro New York 1890-1930* TB/1381
PHILIP RIEFF: The Triumph of the Therapeutic: *Uses of Faith After Freud* TB/1360
ARNOLD ROSE: The Negro in America: *The Condensed Version of Gunnar Myrdal's* An American Dilemma. *Second Edition* TB/3048
GEORGE ROSEN: Madness in Society: *Chapters in the Historical Sociology of Mental Illness. || Preface by Benjamin Nelson* TB/1337
PITIRIM A. SOROKIN: Contemporary Sociological Theories: *Through the First Quarter of the Twentieth Century* TB/3046
FLORIAN ZNANIECKI: The Social Role of the Man of Knowledge. *Introduction by Lewis A. Coser* TB/1372